Always a Winner

on Route 66

by

DON SHINNICK

as told to James C. Hefley

ZONDERVAN PUBLISHING HOUSE
GRAND RAPIDS, MICHIGAN

Dedicated to Marsha
and
my children

Contents

Introduction

by

RAYMOND BERRY

(Former All-Pro offensive end for the Baltimore Colts; Holder of career record for pass receiving in the National Football League. Now an assistant coach for the Dallas Cowboys.)

To each of us there is usually one friend who is "extra special." Don Shinnick is that person in my life. The main reason is that because of his influence I turned to Jesus Christ as my Saviour. As a result, for the first time I experienced a personal relationship with the Living God and came to know His forgiveness, His love, and His daily presence through the ups and downs of life.

Apart from what Don has meant to me personally, I think he is the most outstanding personality I have ever met. The reasons for this are many.

Physically he is impressive, carrying 225 pounds at 6'0". He works hard, studying more than any Colt player I ever knew in preparation for a game during our eleven years together in Baltimore. Don is a great competitor. He plays to win. He can be counted on to be ready when game time comes. This dedication is a big reason why he has intercepted more passes than any linebacker in pro football history.

Don has been gifted with a great mind. He is one of the sharpest guys I've ever known. His sense of humor is incomparable. He also is an independent thinker, often unorthodox, unpredictable, and sometimes a nonconformist. To know him is to be stimulated and challenged to think.

The most important thing about Don Shinnick is his commitment to God through Jesus Christ. No Christian is perfect and neither is Don, but he is a growing Christian, dedicated to letting God's Will be done in his life.

I think you'll agree with me that all these things are true after you have read his autobiography.

Publisher's Preface

We have been enthusiastic about each of the three previous sports autobiographies[1] we have published, but we are especially excited about Don Shinnick's story. Don is not only a well-known football player with twelve years of professional experience, but he is also a popular and capable Christian leader who has spoken to audiences from coast to coast and continues to thrill thousands from the platform as a representative of the Fellowship of Christian Athletes. Loren Young, the FCA's Southeast Regional Director, calls him, "the epitome of what we in FCA would like young athletes to become."

The Baltimore Junior Chamber of Commerce named Don its "Outstanding Young Man of the Year" for 1962 in recognition of his activities both on and off the football field in Baltimore.

Following are the career highlights of his 19-year athletic career.

SAN PEDRO, CALIFORNIA HIGH SCHOOL — THREE YEARS

*Baseball, track, and football standout.
*Named to Los Angeles "All-City" baseball and football teams.

UNIVERSITY OF CALIFORNIA AT LOS ANGELES (UCLA) — THREE YEARS

*Earned a Rugby letter while at UCLA.
*As sophomore fullback, averaged 7.5 yards per carry while playing behind All-American Fullback Bob Davenport.
*His teams won 25 of 30 contests and in 1954 UCLA's famous "eleven from Heaven" team was named National Collegiate Champions by the Football Writers of America after going undefeated in nine games.

---

[1]Steve Sloan, Phil Regan, and Steve Spurrier.

*Associated Press "Back of the Week," November 8, 1956.
*Standout player in 1956 Rose Bowl.
*Starter for 1957 College All-Stars in Chicago.
*Named "Outstanding Lineman" and awarded Spaulding Trophy in the East-West Shrine game following the 1956 season.

U.C.L.A. Quotes

"Shinnick is a natural athlete, a powerhouse who loves the roughgoing." Dick Hyland, *Los Angeles Times*.

* * *

"Shinnick lives up to his nickname of 'The Bull' with his bruising shots inside the tackles." Jack Tobin, *Los Angeles Mirror*.

"If opponents are looking for a reason why UCLA's football team is No. 1 in the nation — outside of the fact that the Bruins can punt, pivot, and pass better than any other eleven — they might consider this heretofore undisclosed asset: *They also pray.* . . . Maybe that's why the 'Eleven from Heaven' can praise the Lord and pass the football like the dickens!" Jeane Hoffman, *Los Angeles Mirror*.

* * *

1956 Rose Bowl: "Shinnick could be labeled the 'hero' of the comeback brigade. He played a great game in stopping the gaps in the left side of the Bruin line." Bill Hollohan, *San Pedro News Pilot*.

* * *

In recapping UCLA's crucial 14-13 1956 win over Stanford, *Sports Illustrated* called Shinnick "easily the outstanding player on the field. (He) shot through the line to block the try for the (deciding) point."

BALTIMORE COLTS — TWELVE YEARS

*Second draft choice of the Colts in the National Football League draft in 1957.

*Member of the 1958 and 1959 Colts' National Football League championship teams.

*United Press Second Team All-Pro — 1959.

*Tied for the National Football League pass interception title in 1959 — a rare accomplishment for a linebacker.

*Leads all pro linebackers in pass interceptions.

*Named "National Football League Defensive Player of the Week" by *Pro Football Illustrated* in 1962, 1967 and 1968.

*Starter on the Colts' defensive squad for the past 12 years during which the Colts have won 115 games, and lost only 51 games and tied three.

*Member of 1964 Colts' Western Conference champions team in the National Football League.

*Member of the 1968 Colts' National Football League championship team.

Reams of sports copy has been written about Don Shinnick. Limited space precludes us from quoting extensively, but here are a few opinions from the sports world.

BALTIMORE COLT Quotes

"Shinnick the deadly." Ogden Nash, Baltimore's most distinguished man of letters in *Life* magazine.

* * *

"Don Shinnick is a football player. He is also a character. And sometimes the two get so mingled it is tough to separate one from the other.

"He leads the Colts in prayer before each game. He also is the blitzing linebacker leader and leading interceptor.

"He is the tranquilizer, but causes stomach spasms, or what you might call belly laughs.

"He is religious, but at the same time irreligious about everything but religion.

"He is the hidden factor who keeps the Colts on their toes for fear of an explosion. He breaks the tension and also breaks up his teammates physically with mirth." Cameron Snyder, *Baltimore Sun*.

"We kid him about his speed, but Don is actually very quick for a few steps at a time. When he first makes his move he's quick, and he has tremendous instincts. That's why he's always around the ball.

"He is great at reading keys and reading the quarterback's eyes. A lot of veterans do that and Shinnick is one of the best. If it looks as though a play isn't coming into his territory, he watches the quarterback's eyes and sometimes that enables him to get to the ball.

"Don has great hands, too. When he gets a shot at an interception, he usually makes it. He's still quite a man to have around. He makes the big play" — Don Shula, head football coach, Baltimore Colts, as quoted by *Baltimore Sun*.

Author's Preface

Beyond the face,
Behind the mask;
What lies there?
I dare to ask —
Can one ever know
Another's mind —
The hidden places;
The infinite dreams
Behind the mask?

That little whiff of verse (whether from me or another bard —
I can't remember) suggests my purpose in writing this book.
I will try to tell you what's behind the mask of Number 66,
one of the Baltimore Colts' starting linebackers for 12 years.
No, they didn't name the famous transcontinental highway after
me. But the way guys try to run over me sometimes, you'd think
I was a highway leading to touchdown city.

Jim Murray, the sports columnist, said that if I ever wrote my
autobiography, I should title it "My War With Football," or "How
I Learned to Stop Worrying and Assumed the Three-Cornered
Stance." Jim thinks the game has dealt unfairly with me and
that I deserve more publicity than I get. I'm not humble enough
to disagree with him, but over the stretch of more than half of
my sweet young life, the game has been good to me. Even if
Red Sanders did move me from fullback to the line after I ran
73 yards through the University of Kansas line in the first college
game I ever played for UCLA.

Another reason for doing this autobiography of an NFL player
who was never elected to the pro bowl (Jim Murray, who keeps
sticking up for me, says the pro bowl wouldn't have me if I had
three arms) is to glorify God. That's the best reason I know for
doing anything worthwhile. I owe a lot to many people both
in and out of football, but I owe the greatest debt to God who

gave me the body and mind to play professional football, and who drew me into a loving and rewarding relationship with Himself. So if after reading my story you are moved to think, "What a wonderful God to have done all this for Don Shinnick," then the effort will have been worthwhile.

The "as told to" means that Jim Hefley, a free-lance author of more than a dozen books, has put my thoughts and records into readable, accurate writing. We worked together at intervals over a period of two years, mostly through personal conversation with his tape recorder eavesdropping. (Jim says one reason the Colts have a great defense is that I talk opponents into exhaustion.) This resulted in 250 pages of manuscript. In addition Jim worked from scrapbooks and clipping files which my wife and my mother (my two biggest fans) compiled. Marsha has never seen Mother's scrapbooks of my before marriage days, so I hope she hasn't censored too much.

My clippings have been made possible by a host of sportswriters, principally in Los Angeles and Baltimore. I thank them all for what they've done to further my career, especially the writers in Baltimore. Maybe the guys have mixed a few quotes, but then after all, no one is perfect.

It would take another book to list all the people who have influenced my life. Some of them are mentioned in the book as they crossed my path. Three organizations, one secular and two religious, have meant more to me than I can adequately put in print; the Baltimore Colts football club with its owner Carroll Rosenbloom and past head coach Weeb Ewbank and present head coach Don Shula; Campus Crusade for Christ with its founder and Executive Director, Dr. William Bright and his wife Vonette; the Fellowship of Christian Athletes (my employer during the off-season) and its Executive Director, James Jeffrey, and Southeast Regional Director, Loren Young.

Finally, I thank Zondervan Publishing House for encouraging me to do this book and for making it available in attractive form.

DON SHINNICK
Baltimore, Maryland

1

"The San Pedro Kid"

Everything and everyone has to have a beginning. I yowled my first complaint in St. Luke's Hospital in Kansas City the year "Red" Grange retired from pro football.

Although I weighed about 215 pounds less then than I do now, the pediatrician said he had never felt such muscles in a baby's shoulders and legs. He also reported that my "tongue was no longer than the Lord allowed and it did not need clipping." Some of today's NFL officials may disagree.

I must have thought kindergarten was sissy stuff at the Mark Twain School in Kansas City. The first four days I pulled a Huck Finn and stayed outside watching a man build a wall. When the teacher caught on and dragged me inside, I moaned like a quarterback who is being shoved toward China by Bubba Smith. Teacher said I had "speech difficulties." The other kids called it something else on the way home. After I taught them some manners Teach inscribed *pugnacious* on my first conduct report.

My folks were divorced when I was two. Five years later mother took my older brother Dick, older sister Shirley and me to San Pedro, California, where she remarried and we spent the rest of our growing-up years. Dad also remarried and lives today in Sun City, Arizona.

Most of the ships coming to Los Angeles tie up at San Pedro's wharves. Many fathers of my school buddies were fishermen or longshoremen. My stepfather ran a hamburger business.

We lived in a red brick and frame house at 1335 West 12th Street, about 20-30 minutes walk from the school, the time depended on whether I had a test or a game coming up. A vacant lot was conveniently located next door, just the right size for

19

football practice and close enough for me to run home for "a drink of water" when the big guys started making hamburger out of me.

I threw 126 *San Pedro Pilot* papers after school and earned the money for my first bicycle. Would you believe — my first injury? I tumbled off and broke a front tooth.

There was a club which required an applying member to write his name with his own blood. I drained enough to fine-line my initials D.D.S. The initials are why some people think I'm the only dentist playing in the NFL. The D.D. really stands for Donald Dee. A sportswriter once called me Dandy Donald Dee. If I hadn't been a peace-loving man, he might have needed a dentist.

There was a gang of older boys who got their kicks from beating up merry little gentlemen. They caught me in the park behind some bushes, but I made like Gale Sayers in heavy traffic and got away. The only time I've run as fast since was during a big rhubarb between the Colts and the Eagles in 1959. The trainer found me under the bench begging the water boy for protection.

I didn't collect stamps or rocks. I just liked sports. So did my brother Dick who is a couple of years older than I. He was better in baseball and I was better in football. Did he ever get mad when I got the first hit off him! When I came up to bat again, I didn't even see the first ball he threw.

We shared a room and slept in bunk beds. About the only thing we could get together on was protecting our older sister Shirley. Woe to anyone who tried to give her a hard time.

Trying to keep up with Dick stirred up a competitive spirit in me. I was always wanting somebody to beat somebody. Captain Marvel, I figured, could beat Superman in a showdown fight and Gene Autry could down Roy Rogers in a gun duel or fist fight. I was always trying to be as good as the guys in the next grade. When I was in the sixth grade, I tried to do as well as the seventh graders and so on. I still operate that way and try to stay one up in any competition.

We both thought Mother worried too much about us. She seemed to be concerned when I coughed out of the wrong side of my mouth and when I tied my shoe strings too tight. And she was great on making us finish a job. We had to sop up every bite on our plates. Our room had to stay cleaner than a Marine barracks ready for inspection at Paris Island.

Every kid changes his want-to-be more than the Chicago Bears have changed quarterbacks in the last couple of years. I first wanted to be a G-man and outsmart criminals. Then I wanted to be a mountain climber and beat everyone to the top of the highest mountain. It was always beat, beat, even with my best friend.

This was Kenneth Ferrier. We had colds at the same time. Once we both had legs in casts in the seventh grade for the same disease — Osgood-Schlatters.

Naturally we liked the same girl, a little brunette named Gloria Ruhl, when we were in the sixth grade. We showed off around her and acted sillier than two cats in an aquarium. We finally fought, but since neither of us could throw the other, we settled on drawing names. I got her name and Kenneth got the blank slip of paper. Then I lost interest in Gloria when the competition was eliminated.

Would you believe I didn't miss a day of school until the ninth grade? Not that I was an Einstein with the books. I struggled to make "C's." But my folks said I had to go, rain or shine, puny or healthy. Now I know this helped me establish discipline so that I never think of missing a day of practice in pro football.

What happened in the ninth grade was that the printing class teacher said something I didn't like and I said a naughty word back and threw some type at him. They suspended me for four days, breaking my perfect attendance record.

And I trailed behind my big brother and sister to a Methodist church. We went to everything they had. When I was 15, someone — maybe it was a Sunday school teacher — suggested I go to a membership class. I did and answered the questions so well they accepted me into the church. It was like being promoted from one grade to another — nothing more. I don't blame the minister, Rev. Fred Ross. Maybe I was more interested in a girl. All I can be certain of now is that I believed in Christ as I did Abraham Lincoln. I said verbally that He was the Lord, but my life didn't show that I believed it.

I never thought myself to be a bad kid. I was the scout type who would help an old lady across the street even with the guys watching. I thought about God regularly on Sunday and sometimes during the week. Once I even felt real thankful. This was at the "Y" pool where I was learning how to swim. I had just swum a lap at the shallow end when someone yelled, "Hey, you're a swimmer." Feeling like an Olympic gold medal winner, I strutted around to the deep end and jumped in. The rest was all glub-a-dub-glub. I felt like the Atlantic Ocean was sitting on my lungs when they pulled me out. I thought of God a little more during the next few days, but after a week I was back in the old carefree groove.

As I've already said, sports grabbed me the most. I was still in grade school when the first nuclear bombs exploded and a lot of other important events happened. But what I distinctly remember above everything else was Enos Slaughter scoring from first base on a single and winning the World Series for the St. Louis Cardinals. That year the Chicago Bears beat the New York Giants 21-14 for the NFL championship with Sid Luckman passing and running for two Bear scores. But I didn't care much about that then because I didn't play competitive football until the tenth grade.

As a pro I've been described as "quick, but not very fast." Actually I started doing fairly well in track back in junior high. I won the 50, 100, and 220-yard dash and placed first in the high jump. As a sophomore, a sports editor said I looked like first class decathlon timber. As a senior, I threw the shot put 51'5" to top the Eastern Marine High School League and I helped San Pedro win the mile relay.

But baseball and football were my two high school loves. I dated only once or twice during high school. It wasn't that the girls didn't like me. I had a curl in the middle of my forehead that some thought "charming." But with sports there just wasn't time to be a ladies' man. I felt then (and still do) that no guy can be good at everything. If you want to excell in one or two activities you have to sacrifice somewhere. It's a matter of priorities.

My brother Dick attended neighboring Narbonne High where

he was good enough to attract a UCLA football scholarship offer and a Pittsburgh Pirates baseball contract. He decided on baseball and pitched one year for the Pirates' farm club in Bristol, Virginia. Just before the next season opened he fractured his left arm in a skiing accident on Mt. Baldy. He stayed out a year, then went back to the diamond for one more season before working his way through UCLA as a photographer's assistant. After a stint in the Army (where he made the All-Army baseball team) he went in business with his old boss. Sister Shirley became a registered nurse, married and had four children. Her firstborn are twins, incidentally. All her kids have names beginning with D, maybe because she liked her little brothers Dick and Donald.

Meanwhile, back in center field for the Pedro Pirates I learned humility in the tenth grade when the Pedro third baseman got six hits in a row while I got none in four times at bat. This was Joe Amalfitano, son of a local Italian fisherman and a buddy of mine. Remember Joe? He did big things for the Chicago Cubs, and later joined Mr. Wrigley's coaching staff.

Just for my humble record, I want to say that I set a school record my junior year for runs scored in a single season of baseball although Joe bested my .317 batting average by 51 points. After Joe finished a year ahead of me and signed with the Cubs, I led the team in home runs, most runs scored, and stolen bases. Naturally without Joe around I was Pedro's "most valuable player" and named to the "All-City (Los Angeles) Baseball Team." Earl Battey, whom I played against, was also "All-City" in Los Angeles for 1952. Earl has since hit a few balls for the White Sox, Senators, and Twins. And would you believe that some baseball scouts talked to me? That I didn't sign is perhaps a good thing. The baseball world might not have been worthy of two great players from San Pedro. As I keep telling my wife after a game when NFL Blockers have tried to reduce me to mush, "I could have been another Babe Ruth." But on second thought, maybe it's better to play 14 games a season instead of 162.

And then I discovered Football!

Football is supposed to have started when an Englishman who

dug up the skeleton of a Dane on an old battlefield began kicking the skull around. Some onlookers thought this a nice pastime and dug up a few more skulls and soon the field was full of flying skulls. Then cow bladders replaced skulls and the sport became less macabre.

Is that why some people think football players are big muscle-bound numbskulls who get their kicks by pushing one another around? I disagree. Compare professional baseball and football players and you'll find that almost all football guys attended college while most baseball players are signed out of high school. Several football "numbskulls" have earned Master's and Doctor's degrees during the off-season.

Now I don't mean to say that you have to be a chemistry teacher's delight to play football. But even high school football teaches you a lot more than how to bring down a running target.

You learn to discipline your body and mind and to keep your temper from causing a team penalty. You learn the necessity of pulling with your team brothers. There's nothing more brotherly than a block thrown to open a daylight for your ball carrier.

And dear mothers if you think twice, you'll realize that tender Johnny is more likely to live long enough to vote by being at football practice instead of racing a car around town. Sure, you hear about the kid who gets a freak injury in a game. But how many more get their heads bloodied in automobiles?

Well, I've been typically out of position from where I started a few paragraphs back — namely, to relate the gripping saga of how I helped the San Pedro Pirates sink the opposition in the briny deep of Southern California football waters.

Had I not been so bugged over baseball, I might have gone out for football before the tenth grade. Until then my only football experience had come on the vacant lot next door and in Boys' Club scrimmages.

I told Coach John Santschi I'd like to be a fullback and he said, "Okay, be on time for practice." I was there and did a lot of yelling and hep-hep stuff. The Pedro sports editor called me "spirited." That the team was "pitiful," he said, wasn't Coach Santschi's fault. "The man has tried, tried until he's blue in the face to get the lackadaisical boys to develop the desire to win."

The coach benched two of his veterans, fullback Rafael Tupaz and halfback Jim "the Wrecker" Decker. He started me in place of Tupaz and I made four long runs that totaled seven yards against Southgate High in the season opener. Then Coach Santschi put in "the Wrecker," who took a reverse from me, broke outside his own right tackle, and was long gone — 65 yards into touchdown land. I was still wondering why I couldn't have done that when Coach Santschi pulled me out and put his regular fullback in. Of course I couldn't understand why he would remove me just when I was beginning to march toward stardom. Later when I had grown up a little, he told me the reason: "You were hitting the holes okay, but you weren't picking up your blockers. You were running over your own people."

The rest of the game belonged to "the Wrecker" who seemed determined to show that Coach Santschi had been wrong in not starting him. Jim looked like Jim Brown running against a third-string pro defense. He rushed for 171 yards and led the Pirates to a glorious victory.

Rafael Tupaz regained his old fullback slot and I played two positions most of the rest of my sophomore season. I sat on the end of the bench and guarded the water bucket. I'm still trying to figure out how Pedro won every game and the league championship — their first in eight years — without me. "The Wrecker" made twelve touchdowns and became the first San Pedro gridder ever to receive the Los Angeles "Player of the Year" Award. But at least my family waved flags for me. Just to show how honest I am, though, I'll confess that I missed five extra-point tries in a 56-0 win over Gardena. The *Los Angeles Examiner* put the record of the first half like this:

Rafael Tupaz (the first string senior fullback) bucked for four to set up the scoring jaunt. Shinnick's conversion try was wide.

Decker shot around left end to the eight from where Ancich completed the journey. Shinnick again missed the conversion.

Decker took a reverse from Tupaz and bolted over left tackle for the TD. *Shinnick's extra point try again went blotto.*

Ancich sauntered 20 yards around right end to climax a 27-

yard march. Once again Shinnick missed the conversion. One
of Gardena's aerials went straight into the arms of Shinnick,
who waltzed 58 yards for the fifth San Pedro TD *of the half.*
And again, the massive fullback (me) *missed the extra point.*

I hope you read the report on that last score where I intercepted and made a touchdown — my first! I made one more
TD later in the season and kicked four extra points. I felt ready
for the Rose Bowl!

Midway in the season Pedro played in the unique Los Angeles
Milk Bowl. I say unique because how else can a team both lose
and win in the same game? Eight teams represented north and
south areas of Greater Los Angeles with two teams playing a
quarter. Our Pedro team lost the first quarter to Van Nuys
6-14, but thanks to our southern partners, the south won 43-26.
What happened to the extra point for Pedro? I missed it, naturally, but this one really wasn't my fault. The pass from center
skittered along the ground. Excuses. Excuses. Excuses. Something else I remember about the 1950 Milk Bowl. The temperature was 111°! I'd rather play in Green Bay at ten below.

Hey! Hey! Pedro's first-string fullback graduated and I made
the regular lineup during my junior year (1951). In the first
two minutes of our first league game I got two scores — both
nullified by the officials. Quack! Quack! On the first, a pass reception, they said the passer was down before he threw the ball
to me. The second time, they called backfield in motion. We
won the game, however, but I didn't get on the score sheet. Tough
luck Shinnick, that was me. But I got two legit touchdowns in
the next game which we won 53-12 in a fog so thick John
Unitas couldn't have made an instrument landing.

We won the third 40-0 and we thought we had won the
fourth league game until we learned the correct time. We were
behind a point and on the opponent's four-yard line with 10 seconds of playing time left and a man injured. We failed to select
our next play while the clock was stopped on the official time
out for the injury. We had no regular time-outs left. The clock
started and we huddled but the touchdown pass was no good

because time ran out just as the ball was snapped. I was on the bench with an ankle injury, but the goof taught me a lesson in mental alertness which I still haven't forgotten.

The injury kept me out of the next two games which Pedro lost. The score of the last one was 72-14 with Inglewood's junior quarterback Ronnie Knox engineering the rout. Ronnie was quite a ballplayer. More about him in the next chapter.

I drowned my sorrows by going to the second annual Pro-Bowl in the Coliseum. It was a rip-roaring, star-studded, water-logged, bone-chilling contest with the rain pouring down.

Sammy Baugh was the goat of the game. He first fell off his chair and got his uniform muddy long before getting into the game in the fourth quarter. Then when he did get in he fumbled four times and had his only pass intercepted.

This must have been the wettest pro game ever played. The winning National Conference All-Stars* had a Waterfield, a Creekmur, and a Sprinkle on their roster.

Meanwhile, Pedro's basketball cagers won their first Los Angeles city basketball championship in 80 years. I wasn't on the basketball team. What would they have done with me on the squad?

My senior football season started with a 7-20 loss. I ran for the Pedro TD and gained 43 of the team's 62 yards from scrimmage. The *Los Angeles Times* called me a battering fullback.

That was only the first game in a strange season. I registered one touchdown in each of Pedro's seven games and one in the Milk Bowl. Although Pedro ended up third in the conference, I made the All-Los Angeles grid team, was voted "Co-Player of the Year" in the Eastern Marine League, and given several other honors. Jon Arnett from Manual Arts' High School was high scorer in the city with 112 points, and the Los Angeles "Player of the Year." Unknown to us then, Jon and I were destined to play against each other many times in future years.

The *Los Angeles Daily News* named me to their Hall of Fame. Bill Griffin, the *News* cartoonist, drew my picture, and columnist

---

*The American and National Conferences became the Eastern and Western Conferences of the NFL in 1953.

Mory Kapp strung up a fence of adjectives that set my head to spinning:

Hand Don Shinnick of San Pedro a 12-pound iron ball and he'll blast the casting well over 50 feet; hand off a football to him and he may rip off 50 yards; pitch him a baseball and he'll wallop it at a long ball .350 clip.

I read it and asked, "Is that me?"

During the just completed grid campaign, the 6-foot green-swardman plunged, passed, sterlingly punted, linebacked and blocked, called offensive and defensive signals, and won such eulogy from rival team coaches as: 'Without Shinnick, San Pedro wouldn't have beaten us.'

But when graduation time rolled around (my class had 223 seniors), the bubble cracked a bit. I lacked one tenth of a point in grade average to qualify for entrance to UCLA. I would have to make that up in junior college.

At the graduation ceremonies a brainy classmate, Othal Lakey, gave a talk titled, "Make the Most of What You Have." "So what if I'm not Einstein," I assured myself. "I can use what God has given me."

Right: Little "Donnie" Dee at six months.

Below: Two years old and I've got my eye on the ball.

The two boys are my big brother Dick and I when I was 10, on the vacant lot next door to our home.

Just average form.

Dick, Mother, I, and sister Shirley
at home in San Pedro.

Dick, Shirley, a girl friend and I
at a Forest Home Sunday school
conference in California.

2

"Turning Point"

The University of California at Los Angeles, better known as UCLA, was a natural choice since it was close by and my brother Dick was already there. The Bruins coaching staff offered me a scholarship on the condition that I come up to UCLA's academic requirements by attending Valley Junior College for a semester. The Bruins even got me a summer job working with their great first-string fullback Bob Davenport.

Bob and I roughnecked for an oil company near Long Beach for $3.00 an hour. The rugged work kept me in shape and gave me the opportunity to get to know Bob, one of the really great college players at that time. That I was a fullback and would be a candidate for his position didn't keep Bob and me from hitting it off.

I sensed right away that Bob was different from any athlete I had ever known. He wasn't super pious. He could joke and laugh as much as the next guy. But he was kind, sincere, and exasperatingly honest.

We had to do a lot of weed cutting. I noticed that Bob always did this dirty job well while I cut corners and goofed around when the boss wasn't around.

One day in a weed patch he told me how he had found reality in life. "I went to church, sang hymns, gave offerings, and even prayed before realizing something was missing," he said. "Then at a church camp I heard that Christ wanted first claim on my life. That bothered me because I knew I had always put sports first. I came home and continued thinking about Christ: who He was, how He had died on the cross, and what He demanded from me. About two weeks later I was looking out the window of my room, when I realized I must make a decision. Right

31

there I asked Christ into my heart. I didn't really understand what happened but I knew He was there. It wasn't until I went to UCLA and got into Campus Crusade for Christ that I started growing as a Christian should — by Bible study, good Christian fellowship, and witnessing. There I realized I could glorify the Lord a little in return for the wonderful new life He had given me."

He stopped and gave me a big brother look. "You should get into Campus Crusade when you get to UCLA. Then you'll understand what I mean."

I thought quite a bit about Bob's testimony but finally decided I was okay as I stood. In August I said good-by to roughnecking and played in two big prep bowl games. The Shrine Bowl pitted top players from southern California high schools against the best picks from schools in the north. We whopped the northerners 20-0. The highly touted Ronnie Knox received "Player of the Game" honors but my line bucks (16 times for a 4.6 yard per try average) set up his terrific pass plays. There were 36,000 people in the Coliseum, my biggest crowd to date.

I set a record in the Southern California College Prep Charity Football Bowl. Not in the playing, although I ran for two touchdowns to help the Los Angeles All-Stars beat the All-Southern California All-Stars 24-13. The record came in the weighing in. At 212 lbs. I was the heaviest back ever to play in the Charity Bowl.

In September I proudly suited up for the Valley Junior College Monarchs. But the coach took the wind from my sails by starting a lighter fullback ahead of me in the first game. He repented and reversed himself in the next game and I got the first touchdown. That game against Santa Monica and the next against a naval team were all glory for me. I bulled (they called me "Big Bull") my way through the line for an average of about six yards per carry. We won both games.

Then just when I was beginning to feel invincible, I had to get a broken thumb and a sprained ankle in a game against Glendale which we lost. I sat and fretted on the bench for the next four games.

Finally I was back in the game against Long Beach. They spelled my name Scinnich in the program. Mike Farguson, the

Long Beach quarterback, had a crazy way of calling signals. Instead of numbers, he would yell a girls' name — "Geraldine," "Patsy," "Beverly," and so on. I fixed him on one play when I was playing defense. Just as he got ready to yell the girl's name, I hollered, "Mary Lou!" We won the game 12-0, perhaps proving that girls should be left out of football.

I had a big imagination back then — and a bigger head some said. My short stories in English Lit had the poor prof crying in his Shakespeare. One began this way:

"I am in the deepest part of Africa, in one of its largest jungles. Don't ask me what jungle, because I do not know. The story I am about to tell you is one you will never forget."

Then after a few episodes of Tarzan stuff, I wrote a spine-tingling climax:

"I have been in the jungle for three days and I am starving. While looking for food and stumbling along, all of a sudden I am being pulled in by the earth beneath me. I could not figure out what it was but now I know. I am trying to hurry this story because in about ten seconds I am going to be swallowed up by quick sand."

I wrote another story about a mountain-climbing expedition during which one of the climbers got a piece of pointed ice stuck in his stomach. "The ice was melting," I wrote, "and slowly but surely he was dying." This guy and two of his buddies lived to climb the mountain and get back down. The story ended thus:

"Now to tell the world that they were the only men to climb this mountain," Bill shouted out. "Just as he did, an earthquake destroyed the world."

The prof called this "highly improbable"! Now you know why I asked a professional writer to help me with this book.

But my grades were good enough to get me admitted to UCLA during the second semester. What a greeting I received. "Sorry, Mr. Shinnick, but the rules say a second semester transfer student can't practice football. You can play Rugby, baseball, badminton — anything, but you can't practice football."

I took up Rugby, also called "English football," where fifteen men on a team play two 40-minute halves on a field similar to football. There are no time-outs except those called by the official to move an injured official or to replace torn pants. And no substitutions are allowed. Points may be scored by kicking or running. The game helped keep the blubber down and kept me in shape for fall football.

UCLA was an exciting place for me. I got to know some talented kids who were studying for movie and television careers. Carol Burnett was then a student on the campus. She played the part of a female coach in the '54 Varsity Show called *Love Thy Coach*. I still don't understand why they didn't select me for a lead part.

UCLA was then in the news for alledgedly sheltering Communist activities. Some called the campus "Big Red." UCLA also had the dynamic movement called Campus Crusade for Christ which had started on the campus back in 1951. Crusade was then moving fast to become one of the most dynamic Christian movements ever to invade big university campuses.

The brains and heart behind Campus Crusade was dapper Bill Bright, a short gentleman with a mustache who looked the part of a well-groomed, articulate professor. Bill was a successful businessman when his mother's prayers steered him to the First Presbyterian Church of Hollywood. There he became personally acquainted with Christ and felt a compulsion to share his new life with others.

While enrolled in nearby Fuller Theological Seminary, Bill organized teams of young Christians to go to skid row, jails, road camps, and other places to introduce down-and-outers to Christ. Then he suddenly realized that few Christians were trying to reach the "up and outers," especially college students. This led him into an unusual experience which I've heard him tell about many times:

"It was a spring night, 1951, in our home in the Hollywood Hills. I was studying for a final Greek examination when God met me in a most illuminating way. That night, a plan for sharing Christ with the collegians of the world was made known and Campus Crusade for Christ was born. My wife, Vonette, and I began to make plans to implement this Commission of the Lord."

Bill and Vonette moved to a home near the UCLA campus and started a 24-hour chain of prayer among Christian students.

He organized the students into teams with the purpose of sharing Christ with every group on campus. In his first meeting at a frat house more than half the men said they would like to have a personal knowledge of Christ. A similar response came from a sorority house where thirty girls committed their lives to Christ. By the end of the year over 250 UCLA students had made commitments to Christ. Though only a fraction of the school's enrollment, they included the student body president, several top athletes, and other student leaders.

Three-time All-American Donn Moomaw was one. The day after Donn intercepted a pass for a winning touchdown to become the hero of a UCLA win over arch-rival USC,* he admitted to Bill Bright, "Football has become my god. If I broke my leg, or for some other reason could no longer play, I would have no reason to live."

That day Donn committed his life to Christ. Soon he became the Campus Crusade Chairman on the UCLA campus. When Donn graduated in 1953, Bob Davenport took over the student chairmanship. The year I enrolled most of the starting football 11 (under Red Sanders starters played both offense and defense) had been won by Campus Crusade. I didn't have a chance of escaping the net. And I'm glad.

At Bob Davenport's urging I began attending Crusade sponsored "College Life" meetings. I heard student testimonies that rang with sincerity and vibrancy. The truth really got to me: Jesus Christ was God-in-flesh. He had died for me. He offered me new life if I would give myself to Him. I faced up to the fact that I had never really committed my life to Christ. I had followed a good-guy way of life but had not experienced LIFE in Christ. I had believed in Christ with my head but not my heart.

What I did was really quite simple. One night I came back to my room after a meeting and prayed, "Lord, I want to have the true belief. I want You to come into my life and be my Master." Maybe I didn't say everything right, but my heart was in it 100 per cent. After that life took on new zest, new

---

*USC — University of Southern California.

joy. I was still my same old wise-cracking self, still a bit of a buffoon, still Don Shinnick — but there was a new Coach in my life.

I won't be surprised that some of you readers will be slamming down this book and maybe saying, "I thought this was a sports autobiography — not religious malarkey. If I want to hear religion, I can go to church."

But I hope you'll stick with me and understand that I can't really tell the story of my life without bringing in Christ. I've never tried to browbeat anyone. Christ doesn't get into a person's life that way. I only want to tell what happened to me so you will understand why I am what I am.

Okay? Still my friend? Then, I'll move into my college football career.

3

"Eleven From Heaven"

Dick Hyland of the *Los Angeles Times* wrote in August, 1954:

> Bob Davenport and Don Shinnick are potentially the best pair of fullbacks in the conference. Davenport appeared greater than ever in spring practice and Shinnick is a natural athlete, a powerhouse who loves the roughgoing.

That sounded great. Only one thing was wrong. Bob, my close friend, was the star veteran, having won "rookie of the year" honors the year before. I was the third-string fullback, behind Doug Peters. If Bob and Doug stayed healthy, I wouldn't get to play much unless Red Sanders shifted me to another position.

When Bob hurt a leg in practice, the imp in me said, "Goody!" But Christ in me said, "Pray that his leg will heal." Christ won out. I asked Bill Bright to join me in prayer; Bob's leg came around.

As a fullback who has to run through and over opposing players, Bob's personal motto was Psalm 18:29: "For by thee I have run through a troop; and by my God have I leaped over a wall."

Bob frequently spoke to youth groups. He earned quick attention and respect by comparing football and faith. As I recall he had three points:

1. As a footballer I must master plays to guide my performance. As a Christian I must learn the plays, or passages, brought out in the Bible to guide my life.

2. Footballers must conform to the edicts of their coaches. Christians must be obedient to God.

3. A footballer must put the theories he's learned in action

before he can establish himself. Likewise, a Christian must practice what he preaches.

The first time I spoke for Christ was in a Campus Crusade meeting at a frat house. I quoted a verse or two of Scripture which I had memorized and said I was glad to be a sure-enough Christian. Good thing I was leaning against a post. I might have fallen flatter than a quarterback under the Rams' Front Four.

September 5 seemed a long time coming — that was the date I could officially scrimmage with the team. Coach Red called our first interteam tussle "the best first scrimmage" since he had been with the Bruins. I thought it was a pretty good workout myself. I scored twice and gained 48 yards in nine plunges. *Collier's* magazine looked two years ahead and picked me among future senior All-Americans.

Red Sanders had lost eight of his eleven starters who had played in the Rose Bowl the previous New Year's day when UCLA lost 28-20 to Michigan State. Conference rules prevented a team from playing consecutive games in the classic. Still *The Saturday Evening Post* said we were not the type of team to lose incentive because of this. The *Post's* sports department said we had "the finest, deepest line in UCLA's history."

This was a team where seven of the starting eleven were members of the Campus Crusade team. A writer called us "the eleven from heaven —" a name that stuck. I wondered where that left our opponents.

But the guys really were top Christians and a smashing answer to people who say Christians are sissies. That charge and the claim that football players are dumb both ruffle my feathers.

Take Primo Villanueva, a Mexican preacher's son, who was 5' 9½" and weighed only about 160 lbs. soaking wet. Primo, the left halfback, was quicker than greased lightning on the breakaway. "Da Preem" as we called him, became a Christian at UCLA. He said, "I know I'm a better football player because Christ is with me." And what a football player "Da Preem" turned out to be in 1954.

Our first game against the San Diego Naval Training Center was just a warmer-upper. We swamped the sailors 67-0. I aver-

aged better than five yards per carry on five rushes and scored
a conversion point when the score was 53-0. I guess they figured
it was safe then for me to kick.

Coach Sanders told us there was no reason we couldn't go all
the way. Knowing that in twelve years as a head coach he had
had only one losing season (the first of his eight years at Vanderbilt before coming to UCLA), we believed him. Drawling
Coach Red then held stubbornly to the old-fashioned single wing
attack formation in which the tailback calls the plays, even
though most coaches were running the Standard-T and the more
recent Sliding-T.

The University of Kansas loomed as our first college opponent.
We expected to trim the Jayhawkers' feathers easily, then move
on to beat mighty Maryland, the nation's number one team in
1953. Beating them would probably put us on top of the national
polls.

I sat on the bench and watched first Davenport, then Decker,
no relation to my old teammate, "the Wrecker," at San Pedro,
then Doug Bradley score against Kansas in the first quarter. I
was still warming the wood when the Bruins were leading 25-7
and a minute to go. The coach said "go get it" and I did. I took
the ball on a spinner and a half, found daylight between tackle
and guard, and ran 73 yards with "elephantine grace" (as one
writer described it) before being tackled on the Kansas 10. I
think the guy that caught me from behind was running the 100
in nine flat. From there, our halfback McDougall scored on the
next play. I hate to think how I would have felt if I hadn't played
those few seconds. My mother and stepfather were in the stands,
having driven all the way from San Pedro to see me play my
first college game.

Coach Sanders had our weights notarized before the big Maryland game because he felt the man who buys a football program
is entited to know. All 44 of us added up to 8,520 pounds. I
came out second heaviest at 220. Jack Ellena carried about three
pounds more.

The game gained national attention because many felt the
winner would end up national champion. The Terps had whipped

Kentucky 20-0 the week before while we had been putting the wraps on Kansas. This was the big game for both of us.

The oddsmakers picked UCLA by three points, perhaps because we were at home. The game proved to be close as predicted.

In a close match, the team that takes advantage of the other's miscues will usually win. Maryland fumbled on a first quarter punt and the Bruins took possession on the Terps' 10. Bob Davenport went over on the second offensive play. But Sam Brown missed the conversion kick — a big, big break for Maryland.

The Terps came back in the fourth quarter to go ahead 7-6. Then we had our second good break when a clipping penalty forced the Terps to kick from their one. A short, bad kick gave us the ball on the 15. Three plays later Davenport drove across the goal for the game-winning score. The Terps coach Jim Tatum said afterwards that the Bruins were the best team he had ever played against. My few minutes of play were completely overshadowed by the tremendous rushes of Bob Davenport. He was so great that I felt good just to be Number 2 fullback behind him. (Red Sanders had moved me up one notch after the Kansas win.)

We went into the next game strutting our stuff and learned a lesson. We were leading 21-0 when the Washington Huskies capitalized on two fumbles and an interception. Suddenly we found ourselves nursing a razor-edge one-point lead with less than three minutes to play. Would you believe Davenport fumbled and the Huskies almost scored again? We came home from Seattle a wiser and more humble team, a winner by only one point.

What did "the kid" do in that game? I carried the ball twice for a total of four yards.

Talk about stings. We got them the following week. The critics who couldn't see us winning the national title said our narrow escape from Washington showed we weren't national contenders.

The stings hurt, but they were good for us.

And bad for poor Stanford which had slapped a 21-20 decision on UCLA the previous year.

Ask John Brodie, now the signal caller for the San Francisco 49'ers, and Paul Wiggin who played defense for the Cleveland Browns. They were among the victims on the blackest day in Stanford history when we massacred the Indians 72-0. Brodie wound up with a minus 17 in rushing.

Just about every Bruin got a piece of the action. Sam Brown, UCLA's fumbling "goat" of the Husky game, ran back two punts for TD's. I had my best college day yet with a 5.33 yard average per carry and a touchdown that was called back for backfield in motion. Without this penalty, the score could have been 79-0. But then, doesn't the Bible say, "Blessed are the merciful"?

Look out, Oregon State Beavers.

They didn't and were chewed up 61-0 by the point-a-minute Bruins. For the second week in a row a UCLA opponent tasted its worst defeat ever.

Hurrah for the Bruins' second-string fullback — me. I got my first college touchdown on a mighty one-yard gallop against the Beavers. Excuse my modesty, but I rushed for 56 yards (seven per carry), six yards more than my buddy Bob Davenport.

On to Berkeley moved the mighty Bruins.

We played nice, real nice and came away on the long end of a 27-6 score. "Da Preem" (Primo Villanueva) passed and ran for 233 yards. Davenport gained 89 yards. What I did isn't worth mentioning, except I kept my record intact of never having been thrown for a loss.

On the way back someone called Villanueva, "Wetback." The little Mexican laughed and said, "If I'm a wetback, then Coach Sanders is an immigration officer."

Forward, mighty Bruins.

We next defeathered the University of Oregon Ducks 41-0.

Then came the University of Southern California Trojans. We felt charitable to our cross-town neighbors and didn't score but one TD until the fourth quarter.

The Trojans were on our eight, when as their coach, Jess Hill, said later, "the dam broke." Jim Decker intercepted a pass and went for 96 yards. A clipping penalty nullified the score, but from there on we stepped on the gas. The final score for our last game of the season was 34-0.

Undefeated and untied, we won the Pacific Coast conference. The Trojans, one of our victims, finished second in the conference and went to the Rose Bowl. A UCLA rooter didn't help their morale by hanging out a sign during the final game that read: "WE'RE SENDING SC TO THE ROSE BOWL."

Though we didn't get to smell the roses, we received plenty of other honors. Both the United Press International coaches poll and the Football Writers of America voted us No. 1 with Ohio State No. 2. The writers award entitled us to receive the first Grantland Rice Memorial Trophy. The misguided Associated Press poll put Ohio State first. Five of our guys (Jack Ellena, Jim Salsbury, Sam Boghosian, Primo Villanueva, and Bob Davenport) made the All-Coast first team. My record as a sophomore sub showed I had played 89 minutes, carried the ball 28 times, gained 210 yards, and had a net 7.5 yards average per carry.

Hey, I forgot the coach. Red Sanders was named "Coach of the Year." He had been runner-up to Jim Tatum of Maryland the year before. The old single wing master really deserved it.

Naturally the football world did a great deal of rehashing the season with various sports writers pointing out our strengths and other reasons for winning. I said then and I say again now that our greatest reason for winning was that seven of the starting eleven and three of the second-string were unquestionably committed to the leadership of Jesus Christ. I don't think any of us thought of our faith as a magic talisman. But because we followed Christ, we played harder, worked together better, and won.

How better could I close this chapter than by quoting some of their testimonies:

TERRY DEBAY — Quarterback
(American Legion Trophy for
UCLA's Most Valuable Player — 1954)

When I was 11 years old, I went to church and heard for the first time in a very unemotional way that I needed a Power greater than myself to direct my life. I was told that this

Power was Jesus Christ. By accepting Him as Saviour I was told that my life would take on new meaning. In 10 short years my life has blossomed into a wonderful experience. It has proved to me that Christ is real in the game of football and the game of life.

BOB DAVENPORT — Fullback
(All-American)

Playing football on a great team such as UCLA's is truly a privilege and a thrill. But there is a greater team than our Bruin club or any other ball club. That is the great Christian team. The Bible promises anyone who follows plays that Christ calls, the greater life this world can offer, plus an eternal life with Him.

JACK ELLENA — All-American Tackle
(UCLA Football Athlete of the Year — 1954)

Religion, if it is accepted by a person, does two things. First, it makes a difference in the daily living of an individual. Second, it holds him steady in times of strife.

PRIMO VILLANUEVA — Tailback
(Most improved player and outstanding senior — 1954)

Being a Methodist preacher's son, I have always gone to church on Sunday, but that was almost all it amounted to until recent years. And it wasn't until this year, associating with other Christians on the UCLA football team and attending some 'Crusade for Christ' meetings that I realized that a Christian's life must be an every day, every minute, every second affair.

BOB HEYDENFELDT — End

I feel that my life has been motivated by something much more powerful and satisfying than a football game. This motivation is Christianity. Football has been a secondary drive of my life. But it has given me numerous opportunities to tell students how Christianity can be applied to every day life. I am glad to have a God who cares for one so insignificant as I. Christianity is to me what a football is to a footgall game — indispensable.

CLARENCE NORRIS — End

> Prayer never fails. All that one needs is to pray earnestly as
> though he expected everything from God. Then one should
> work faithfully as if he expected everything from himself.

P.S. The Baltimore Colts had a big year in 1954, too, though
they didn't realize it. After finishing fourth in the Western Conference Division of the NFL, they laid three important planks
in building for a championship. They got Alan "The Horse"
Ameche from Wisconsin, L. G. (Long Gone) Dupre from Baylor, and Raymond Berry, whom many thought too light for pro
ball, from SMU.

4

"Where Do I Go From Here?"

Nine of eleven Bruin starters graduated in '55 leaving only wingback Jim Decker and fullback Bob Davenport to beef up the juniors and sophomores. Yet Maryland's Jim Tatum, who was anticipating a rematch with us the second game of the season, said, "Red Sanders will lose no one he needs."

Tatum meant that UCLA had depth. Davenport and Doug Peters were two of the best fullbacks in the business. Doug Bradley was available to replace Primo Villanueva at tailback with the sensational Ronnie Knox to back him up. I had seen Ronnie perform for Santa Monica High where he had broken the school's scoring records. After graduation, Ronnie had enrolled at the University of California in Berkeley, then had transferred to UCLA because his father had fallen out with the UC coach. At least, that's what the newspapers said.

The Bruins had less depth in the line, having lost the past season's starting tackles, guards, center, blocking back, and linebackers. So right after spring practice began, Coach Sanders ran his eye up and down my 220 and said. "Shinnick, you'd like to play more, wouldn't you?"

I thought of the 89 total minutes of action I had seen the last season and nodded. He smiled and said, "Good. We'll make you a guard. That's where we need you most."

I knew that Coach Red had two good fullbacks in Bob Davenport and Doug Peters. I sure wanted to play more than 89 minutes this season even if I didn't carry the ball. So I became a guard.

Man, was I green in practice. I was suckered, bounced from side to side, pushed over, and run over. An observing writer called me "a lost lamb." I suffered, but when we came to play

Texas A&M in the season opener, I felt confident I could do the job.

The UCLA — A&M contest pitted Coach Sanders against his former assistant at Vanderbilt, Bear Bryant. Bear's Texans lost 21-0, thanks to a sensational passing display by our second-string tailback Ronnie Knox. Frank Finch of the *Los Angeles Times* said Ronnie lofted his passes a la Otto Graham and rifled them like Dutch Van Brocklin. With his father smiling from the stands, Ronnie completed six of eight, with three going for touchdowns. Coach Sanders was really high on Ronnie. "He could become the greatest tailback ever at UCLA," he exulted. "Never have I seen a cooler man back there." A *Dallas News* writer avowed that Ronnie was worth more than his brother, Fort. And when asked the turning point of the game, Bear Bryant drawled, "When Papa Knox transferred Ronnie from UC to UCLA."

I thought I had done pretty well in this my first league game as a guard until after we returned to UCLA and the coaches called me into the office. But instead of complimenting me, Red Sanders said:

"Do you know, Mr. Shinnick, that if Mr. Brown (Jim Brown, the UCLA left guard, not the great Cleveland back) had not been next to you in that game, they would have gained a thousand yards down the middle? You were not in on any tackles. Now, what do you have to say for yourself?"

This was one of the few times in my life when I was at a loss for words. I finally mumbled something like, "I never played guard before and I'll do better next Saturday."

The next Saturday was *the* game of the year when we flew across the country to tackle Maryland. Because we had beaten them by a touchdown the year before, they were high for revenge.

Maryland writers had been busy quoting Papa Harvey Knox on what he expected Ronnie to do: "They'll think lightning hit 'em. Why, if Ronnie doesn't throw for five or six touchdowns, I'll disown him. I'll cream him." This undoubtedly stirred up the Maryland players to pull out all the stops on Ronnie.

A drenching rain didn't dampen the enthusiasm of the sellout crowd. Just for this game Maryland had added 11,000 bleacher seats. There was a "knock Knox" fan in almost every one.

What happened?

UCLA took the ball to the Terps one-foot line in the first quarter where Doug Peters fumbled. Actually I caused the fumble by failing to block my man. But Maryland didn't get their only touchdown until the third quarter. Which was enough since we didn't score. The shutout broke a 45-consecutive game record in scoring.

Ronnie was good and bad, mostly bad. He completed nine of 12 passes for 96 yards. But he threw two interceptions and was all but eaten alive several times by rushing linemen. The Maryland fans made it rough also for him. They chanted, "Knock, Knock, Knock. We want Knox." And when he left the field, they yelled, "Bring him back."

The statistics were horrible. We had a -21 yards rushing. I played 36 minutes with sore ribs. But all I remember was the mud and that big red Maryland line that kept coming at us like a dragon breathing fire. It was my first trip to Maryland and at that time I didn't care much about returning.

Some say this was the most important game in UCLA history. I don't know about that, but if we had beaten the Terps I think we would have won the national title for 1955.

The sports writers hovered around Harvey Knox after the game. He gave them some juicy quotes about how he would have played the game. Coach Sanders said nothing in return.

My performance in the Maryland game brought criticism that I was "too nice." Coach Sanders dropped me to third-string.

What often follows a big defeat happened to UCLA the following week. We shellacked Washington State 51-0. Ronnie Knox had a bruised shoulder and didn't play. We took Oregon State next 38-0. Ronnie and Sam Brown alternated at tailback. Ronnie passed for one touchdown and showed real talent. But after the game the papers quoted his father as forbidding Ronnie to play against Stanford the following week because of his injured shoulder.

The UCLA athletic director jumped in with the comment, "If a father starts telling a boy when he can play, maybe it's time for the boy to quit football." The UCLA team doctor said Ronnie was in shape to play.

Papa Harvey told the eager-beaver writers that Ronnie had three big money bids already in from the pros and added that he hoped Ronnie wouldn't make football his career since he was grooming for acting.

Coach Sanders was quoted as calling Harvey's remarks, "Unnecessary."

The papers carried the yak-yak over whether or not Ronnie would play right up until game time. As it turned out he did nothing but punt.

We were wary, knowing Stanford would be out to revenge the 72-0 bombing we had dumped on them the year before. Caution didn't seem necessary during the first few minutes because the Indians acted like patsies. We scored each of the first three times we got the ball. But John Brodie brought them roaring back in the second half and almost got our scalps. The game ended 21-13 with Brodie and company on our three

We dumped Iowa 33-13 the following week. Sam Brown and Ronnie Knox alternated at tailback. Sam made three touchdowns on the ground, tying a school record. Ronnie delivered some great plays and also scored. His father was at the game, but if he had anything to say to the sports writers, they didn't quote him.

Ho hum.

We walked over the Bears from Berkeley 47-0. They connected on only six of eighteen passes, and half of these fell into Bruin hands. Ronnie Knox looked like Doak Walker, Otto Graham, and Dutch Van Brocklin all wrapped into one. I played less than half the game.

The next win, 34-0 over the College of the Pacific, was also easy. The points made us the national scoring leader among major colleges with 249 points in eight games. Ronnie Knox completed four out of four passes, two for touchdowns, and was the top Bruin ground gainer. He also made an 82-yard quick kick.

Then we came out of hibernation.

Against the Washington Huskies, whom we had beaten by

only one point the previous year, rocketing Ronnie fractured a bone in his right leg the first time he carried the ball. We moved on without him and scored first. But in less than six minutes the pesky Huskies mushed back and nipped us with two touchdowns. At the half they led 14-7.

Another Husky field goal made the tally 17-7, then Bob Davenport — he had been injured — came in and whammo! Bob's blocking and running helped us move within three points of the Huskies.

With about a minute left the Huskies incurred a delay of game penalty that pushed them back to their own five with a fourth down. Steve Roake, their quarterback, elected to take a deliberate safety, giving us two points, and making the score 17-16, but enabling him to kick from his own 20-yard line. This strategy didn't help them. We moved back to within field goal distance and Jim Decker punched the ball through with 17 seconds to go.

This left only Southern Cal. on our season agenda. By beating the Trojans, we could cinch a Rose Bowl bid.

Jon "Jaguar" Arnett was SC's quarterback. A junior, Jon had been nicknamed "Jaguar" by his frat brothers. After he later became a famous All-American, his roommate did a cute trick. The roomie emptied Jon's bureau drawers and closet and piled all his belongings around the room. Then he hung a sign on the door advertising the room as the "Jon Arnett Museum." No-one ever did that to me.

Well, "Jaguar" almost became a big name in 1955. With over 95,000 fans in the Coliseum, he took the opening kickoff and ran it back 97 yards. But his team was off side and we got to kick again. We won 17-7 with Sam Brown and dependable Davenport coming off with the ball-carrying honors.

The win made UCLA Pacific Coast champions for the third straight year. This time we could go to the Rose Bowl. Our opponent: a rematch with Michigan State, the Big Ten champs, and the team that had defeated the Bruins two years before.

At the first postseason drill Coach Sanders called me over. I told him that I thought I could play linebacker better than guard, but he didn't move me then.

On December 17 we got a lift when Ronnie Knox appeared for a light workout. He looked as if he might be able to play.

Just before the big New Year's game the combined UCLA and Michigan State teams enjoyed a big sports dinner. Dean Martin, Jerry Lewis, Kay Starr, and Ronald Reagan, the future governor of California entertained us. The Michigan State guys may have been impressed, but with UCLA next door to Hollywood movie stars were old stuff to us. Maybe we were heroes to the stars. I don't know because none of the cast asked me for my autograph.

If you ask me, Duffy Daugherty, the Michigan State Coach, is hard to beat as an entertainer. He always comes up with a good one. One I like — (I think he told it on Jack Benny's show before the game) — was about the time a Michigan State ballplayer lost the seat of his pants to a Minnesota tackler. The State boy kept on running, hanging onto the football with one hand and holding up what was left of his pants with the other. After he scored, his teammates formed a circle around him so he could put on a new pair of pants. Duffy yelled from the sidelines, "That's the best showing you've made all year!"

The Bruins, of course, were remembering the 28-20 defeat to the Spartans two years previous and wanted to make a better showing this time. Only one big name sports writer picked us to win. One who picked State said it would be deception over power. Another who picked State said, "I have too much respect for Morrall." This was none other than Earl Morrall, the Colts "Super Sub" of 1968. Earl had completed 42 of 68 passes during the 1955 season and looked formidable to us. We were also worried about State's right and left halfbacks, Kowalczyk and Peaks, who together had averaged six yards per carry.

The 1956 Rose Bowl game has to be one of the biggest thrills of my life. The Rose is the queen of all the bowls, the oldest, the largest in audience, and the classiest. Twenty men who played for Washington State and Brown in the first of the modern Rose Bowl series back in 1916 were special guests for this game. One happened to be Wallace Wade, who had played guard for Brown, and later coached three Alabama teams and two Duke elevens into the Pasadena classic.

The big moment finally came and we kicked off to the Spartans. Earl uncorked a pass on the first play of the game — right into our Jim Decker's happy hands. Jim returned the ball to the Spartan 16 and four plays later Bob Davenport went over from the two. The game was less than three minutes old and we could taste victory already.

The Spartans tied it at 7-7 in the second quarter when Earl passed to Clarence Peaks for a score. They went ahead 14-7 in the fourth on halfback Clarence Peaks' flip (he hadn't passed for a score all year) to John Lewis. UCLA hadn't given up two aerial scores in any game of the past season.

But Ronnie Knox brought the Bruins back and it looked as if the game might end in a tie. About this time southern California was shaken by an earth tremor. Most people in the stadium probably thought it was only a bone-jarring tackle.

Then began two of the most confusing minutes I've ever seen in a football game. Five penalties were called in the final minute and 34 seconds.

After Michigan State's Gerald Planutis missed a field goal, we took possession on our own 20. Suddenly a Big Ten official signalled a penalty: 15 yards against UCLA. The official claimed Assistant Coach Jim Meyer had gone beyond the side line restraining line. That put us on our five from where Ronnie retreated deep into the end zone, was almost tackled, and threw a short pass which landed in the field of play. The ball touched an ineligible receiver and drew another penalty that put us on the two and a half yard line.

Ronnie got off a short but high kick. Peaks moved under it at the UCLA 34 but did not signal for a fair catch. Hardiman Cureton, our right guard, ran past Peaks, yanking him by the arm while the ball was still in the air. Peaks didn't make the catch, but Cureton's yank drew an "interference with the opportunity to catch the ball." The 15-yard penalty put the ball on our 19.

The Spartans then fumbled, recovered and were penalized back to the 30 for pushing. They gained 11 yards on two plays, then were penalized for delay of the game back to our 24. With seven seconds left Dave Kaiser who hadn't kicked a field goal all season and who left his contact lenses on the sidelines came in and booted the three-pointer that won the game for Michigan State. But to further show the confusion, the press box was told Planutis had kicked the winning field goal. Not until 25 minutes after the game was over did the press learn that Kaiser was the hero.

You can bet that UCLA people howled about the penalties, especially the 15-yarder called against Coach Meyers. The *Daily Bruin* (UCLA's campus newspaper) sports editor reported with obvious sarcasm that the official had been given a letterman's sweater at Michigan State. But another paper recalled how UCLA had won a game the past November 12 with a field goal in the last 18 seconds and added, "Those who live by the foot will eventually get kicked in the teeth."

About all I can say is that Michigan State got the breaks in that Rose Bowl game and the benefit of what seemed to be a bad call.

Naturally my sweet Momma combed the newspapers for comments about my playing. She didn't find much except for a line or two by a San Pedro writer. Bill Hollohan called me the hero of UCLA's comeback brigade and said that I had played a great game in stopping the gaps in the left side of the Bruin line.

I thought I played a good game at guard. I was just getting used to the position.

I even thought the pros might become interested in me — *if* I could play more my senior season.

5

"Half Right and Half Wrong"

I wondered what new position Red Sanders would switch me to during my senior season. As a sophomore third-string fullback, I had played less than 90 minutes all season. As a junior guard on offense and defense, I had played more, but inexperience at this position kept my frustrations up. I knew I needed to start and finish every game during my last year if I was to interest the pros.

This I expected to do until the Pacific Coast Conference rules committee dropped their bomb.

The *Oakland Tribune* lit the fuse with a story that charged UCLA varsity football players with receiving $35 above the $75 monthly for 50 hours work permitted by PCC rules.

Tommy Protho, the head coach at Oregon State who had worked under Red Sanders, immediately came to UCLA's defense. He stated that while he was at UCLA no athlete had received any more than his actual school expenses.

The conference rules committee began an investigation. They found that UCLA players had each been receiving $50 for work on campus plus $60 from an alumni fund for work supposed to be done off campus. Several other schools were paying only $75 per month, the cash amount authorized by PCC rules, *plus giving room and board on campus* which was not available at UCLA. So actually some schools were paying more than UCLA.

Tommy Protho was then quoted as saying flatly, "Conference rules are at fault. Any conference that operates this way will have everybody circumventing the rules."

Sportswriters supporting UCLA charged the other schools with hypocrisy. *True* magazine ran a long exposé article about payoffs given by PCC schools to outstanding high school athletes. I don't know whether all the charges were true or not. I do know what I had been receiving. And I did wonder about the motives of some of the Conference committee members from schools that had been losing football games to UCLA during the past few years. A writer put UCLA's suspicions in print: "Some who can't beat UCLA on the football field are trying to win at the conference table."

Those of us whose careers were on the line held our breaths awaiting the ruling of the Conference fathers. They finally reprimanded Red Sanders and limited each senior to playing half the 1956 season or five consecutive games. Did this mean they thought us half right and half wrong?

Coach Sanders had already lost 17 last-year lettermen by graduation. The penalty meant that he would lose half the time of ten seniors. But he took it in stride, even joking at a party that the "R" in his name no longer stood for "Red" but for "Reprimand."

Ronnie Knox was the best-known of the ten seniors. He and his talkative Papa surprised no one by taking off to Canada. Another UCLA player, Tommy Adams, also signed a Canadian contract.

The eight of us who remained talked the situation over with Coach Sanders. The decision was that Bob Bergdahl and Doug Bradley would play games one through five, the others, three through seven. One other senior and I picked six through ten. Bergdahl would be the blocking quarterback for the first five games and I would play this position, a new one to me, plus linebacker, also new to me, on defense for five games.

Those first five weeks were really tough for me. I wore the bench out for four games, then during the fifth I went up to the spotting box and watched. The guys did well. They beat Utah, Oregon, Washington State, and UC at Berkeley. They lost only to Michigan which had the great Ron Kramer.

My time *finally* came against Oregon State. Although the Beavers hadn't crossed the UCLA goal line in five years, they were favored by one point. Red Sanders was pitted against his former assistant Tommy Protho. Well, at least Tommy proved Coach

Sanders' a good teacher. Comment after the game was that I was cold, leaned a bit into my blocks, and needed to get warmed up. I did get off a 68-yard punt. But we lost 21-7.

The next game with powerhouse Stanford was the last for the four seniors who had been chosen to play games three through seven. Stanford's ball-handling quarterback John Brodie was leading the nation in total offense. He and senior tackle Paul Wiggin, were being puffed for All-American honors. The team had their eyes on the Rose Bowl and naturally, wanted to avenge the 72-0 drubbing we had given them two seasons before.

Before the game Coach Sanders predicted we would whip Stanford. He added a quote from Shakespeare: "Thrice long is the arm whose cause is just." He may have had in mind Stanford's part in assisting the five-game penalty on his seniors.

Poor Brodie. First he fumbled and set us up for a score. Then our Hal Smith blocked his punt. Pete O'Garro caught the ball as it came down and raced 42 yards for a second TD. I kicked the point after touchdown, making the score 14-0. Early in the second half Brodie narrowed the gap to 14-13. But I blocked the conversion try and we held them until the gun sounded. Altogether, Brodie lost 74 yards to our pass rushing as we fed him a hearty meal of turf.

I learned a lot about linebacking in that game. Positioned between the defensive line and the deep backs, the three linebackers (right, middle, and left) must be ready for whatever the opposing offense develops. When a pass seems likely, they may blitz the quarterback or scoot back to block the throwing lanes and maybe get an interception. On a run, they try to get through the opponent's blockers and tackle the ball carrier. The ideal linebacker is a combination of whirling dervish and Mack truck with a computer brain.

Well, neither we linebackers nor anyone else on UCLA's defense needed a computer brain to figure out what Brodie was going to do on most plays. We just watched his feet.

If he drew his left foot back a little, we looked for a straight fadeback pass or a fullback draw up the middle; if his right foot went back, we anticipated a pitchout or rollout pass; if his feet were even, we looked for a running play outside or an angle-in-pass to the left.

Every time we figured a pass play was coming, we yelled OMAHA and put on the rush. And after the game was over we went to the dressing room, we yelled OMAHA loud enough to break windows five miles away. Well, almost. But you should have heard the yell when I learned the AP had named me "back of the week."

Where did we get our information on Brodie's feet? From watching films of previous Stanford games.

Stanford didn't make it to the Rose Bowl that year. But Brodie and Wiggin have long since proven their playing ability in the pros. Naturally, I'll never let Brodie forget our college game as seniors. All I have to do is yell OMAHA when the Colts play the Forty-niners.

We beat the Washington Huskies 13-9. The key play came in the second quarter after we punted to their one-yard line (I always say we when another team member does a good job. For the record, the punter this time was Kirk Wilson).

The Huskies dropped back to kick. We pushed their quarterback to where the punted ball hit him. I fell on the ball on the two. Three plays later I went in for the touchdown, then I kicked the extra point. I got the game ball!

The next week we beat Kansas 13-0.

I'd almost rather not mention the last game. USC beat us 10-7. The winning margin came on a field goal in the fourth quarter by Ellis Kissinger who had never kicked a field goal before.

Now if I had been a few inches closer, I might have blocked that kick and been a hero. Even after USC chalked up 314 yards running to our 23.

But might-have-beens don't count. There were some who said I *might have been* All-American had I played all ten games as a senior. At least I made *honorable mention* on the Pacific Coast Conference list and second team quarterback on the International News' Services' All-Far-West team. John Brodie was INS' first team quarterback. Did they look at his feet? I can honestly say I wasn't jealous of John. He deserved the honor. When flat on his back, he's still one of my favorite quarterbacks.

But watch how you move your feet, John.

My playing days for UCLA were over, but coming up was the NFL draft and the East-West Shrine Bowl contest.

Before 1955 the NFL had made its 30 rounds of player selections at the annual owners' meeting in mid-January. But early winter bidding by Canadian clubs had forced the League to schedule at least four rounds in November. The present American Football League did not become involved in draft competition until 1960.

The way the draft worked then and now is quite simple. Players are chosen in rounds with each team having one selection per round. The team with the poorest record gets first choice in the round, the next poorest team gets second choice and so on. Teams having identical records toss coins to see who goes ahead.

This time an out-of-the-hat drawing for a bonus pick was made before the drafting began. Green Bay drew the right to select any graduating college football player in the nation. The Packers selected Paul Hornung, the All-American quarterback from Notre Dame.

The first draft round began with the Rams, who got to choose first since they had the poorest record the previous year. They took Jon Arnett. The Forty-niners came next and took John Brodie, whom many felt was destined to become a greater quarterback than Otto Graham. The Colts chose seventh and took the All-American tackle Jim Parker from Ohio State. I mention the other first-round choices to show you the selection of top talent available in 1956. (This made me — a second-round choice — look better.) Besides Hornung, Arnett, Brodie, and Parker, the first round included Ron Kramer (Michigan end to Green Bay), Len Dawson (Purdue quarterback to Pittsburgh), Jim Brown (Syracuse halfback to Cleveland), Clarence Peaks (Michigan State halfback to Philadelphia), Don Bosseler (Miami fullback to Washington), Jerry Tubbs (Oklahoma center to the Chicago Cardinals, later the St. Louis Cardinals), Del Shofner (Baylor halfback to New York), Bill Glass (Baylor guard to Detroit), and Earl Leggett (LSU tackle to the Chicago Bears). Every one of these men have had long pro careers, some (you pick 'em) will probably make the Hall of Fame.

The second round had some pretty good guys, among them Milt Plum, Abe Woodson, John Gordy, and Don Shinnick. The Colts drafted me number two behind Jim Parker, who isn't a bad guy to be behind anywhere.

Only one other UCLA senior besides me was in the first four draft rounds. Would you believe — Ronnie Knox, who had come back from Canada. The story I read was that howls filled the room when Commissioner Bell called out Ronnie's name as the Chicago Bears' third draft choice. "Will you draft Papa Knox, too?" someone asked Papa Bear George Halas. Halas was supposed to have smiled and said nothing in reply. Seriously, however, everyone knew that Ronnie had talent.

Because none of the draft choices could sign until the post-season games ended, there remained a lot of suspense over whether some of the players would accept Canadian offers. Also, some thought I would go to Canada where they still do not play pro ball on Sunday.

The East-West Shrine Bowl game brought together many of the unsigned players chosen in the top draft rounds. Paul Hornung quarterbacked the East team that included big Jim Parker and many more good players. John Brodie led the West with Jon Arnett as a running back, Paul Wiggin at right tackle, me as a right linebacker, and some other great guys.

Our West team was a little fearful before the game. We knew the East outweighed us with some of the best players in the nation. I suggested, "Let's pray together before the game." The guys agreed and I led them in prayer. Several guys said after the game that having prayer together really helped.

Our West squad scored first from a Brodie to Pete O'Garro pass. Then I intercepted a Hornung pass. The East got the ball back and Hornung and company moved to our one-foot line. With fourth down and seconds to go before the first half ended, Paul tried a quarterback sneak. I hit him at the handoff. He fumbled and Jerry Liston of Utah recovered for the West.

Midway in the fourth period the East scored on a 35-yard screen pass from Hornung to Abe Woodson. Oops! Jerry Liston and I barrelled through to deflect Paul's conversion kick and a few minutes later the hard-fought game ended 7-6 for the West. I was glad to come out with only a cut eyelid that required six stiches to sew back together.

Hornung, a really great player, showed good stuff. He passed for 167 yards, only ten less than John Brodie. But Brodie was named "Player of the Game" with Jon Arnett (the West's leading ground gainer) as runner-up. I was named "outstanding lineman" and awarded the Spaulding Trophy.

With the Shrine game over, the moment of contract decision was upon me. The Colts flew me and my mother and stepfather to Baltimore. We talked with General Manager Don Kellett and Coach Weeb Ewbank. They offered me a contract and I told them (and later the press) that I would return home and decide the next Saturday between the Colts and a Toronto offer. I had already decided that Sunday playing would not be an issue. I'll give my reasons for this later in the book. Actually, Cameron Snyder, who still writes sports for the *Baltimore Sun,* had called me right after the drafting and asked if I would play football on Sunday. He knew that Donn Moomaw, a student for the ministry, had turned down the NFL in favor of Canada because of Sunday playing. I told Cameron then that I had no objection to playing on Sunday.

Hamp Pool, the Toronto Coach, found out I had gone to Baltimore. He sent an assistant coach to bird-dog me. This assistant got a room in the same hotel where my folks and I were staying. By some sharp sleuthing he learned I was leaving without signing the contract. The assistant called Coach Pool and when we landed at L.A., guess who was there to welcome us home? Hamp Pool. He took us to dinner and talked contract. "I'll put your contract in a separate envelope from the Colt offer," I told him. "I'll think the offers over, make my decision, and tell no one until the club I select has my signed contract on their desk."

At this stage a sportswriter sharpie in L.A. got involved. He called a Toronto paper and said I had signed for Toronto. He even put someone on the phone who claimed he was me to "verify" the yarn. The Toronto paper printed this false story. Next day the Colts announced that my signed contract had arrived. The slick writer glibly tried to get off the hook by saying that just as I was about to drop the Toronto contract in the mail, the Colts sent an increased offer which I decided to accept. Baloney! It's guys like this L.A. sportswriter who give black eyes to the honest writers.

And Ronnie Knox? He joined the National Guard and began six months of active duty . . . and kept Papa Bear waiting in suspense. Papa Bear didn't disown him, though. He kept hoping that Ronnie would sign later. And one or two stubborn writers repeated what had been said by some since Ronnie was in high school — that Ronnie could become the greatest passer who ever lived.

But my contract was signed and I was looking forward to training camp with the Colts come July.

Meanwhile (as I'll relate in the next chapter), a stronger interest than football tackled me.

The girls carried my books at Valley Junior College.

A playing shot of me at UCLA where I played fullback, linebacker, and blockingback in Red Sanders' single wing system.

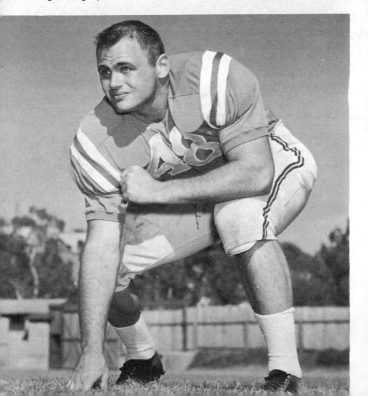

A game with UCLA. I'm number 48 leading the "charge of the light brigade."

Don't I look sweet here after I just signed my pro contract? Maybe it was the curl in the middle of my forehead that hooked Marsha.

6

"The Girl"

"Hey, Hey!" I chuckled aloud as I read the ad in the *Daily Bruin*:

WOULD YOU LIKE TO ESCORT MOVIE STAR MARGARET O'BRIEN TO THE JUNIOR PROM? TELL WHY IN 25 WORDS OR LESS.

With my last college football season over, I didn't see why I shouldn't think more about another sport — dating. And why not start at the top?

So having nothing better to do, I entered the contest by writing: "Dear Margaret, I would like to have the privilege of dating you. I do not know anything about movies, I would like to ask you some questions."

Would you believe? I won.

My first thought when I saw Margaret was: *She has really grown up.* I had seen her as a child star in the movies, but now she was 18.

We had several other dates — how many I don't remember. But I do remember that she was sweet and unselfish and didn't talk about herself all the time.

Bye, bye, Maggie; hello, Marsha.

I had said my first hello to this brown-haired cutie with knockout hazel eyes at a frat party. Gary Lockwood, a former UCLA football teammate, introduced us. (Gary later starred in television's *Lieutenant* series and in real life married the girl who played the lead in *The Girl From Uncle*.) But that was back during the end of the '56 football season and I didn't think again about Marsha Tatlow, an education major and recent Valley Junior College queen, until I saw her at a Campus Crusade

College Life meeting a few weeks after my prom date with Margaret O'Brien.

I emceed the meeting, welcomed the visitors (which included Marsha), and introduced a Moody film on science and Christianity titled *For Time and Eternity*.

As the newly-elected Chairman of the UCLA Campus Crusade movement, one of my duties was to make sure visitors were greeted personally. I took a special interest in Marsha and asked her if she had *time* for a coffee date.

Well, she drank coffee. I had punch and looked her over. Not bad. Not bad.

She didn't look like a painted doll. I liked that. After a few more dates I found out other things. She had a sweetness about her that other girls did not have. She seemed to pay attention to me at parties and not look around to see who was looking at her.

A couple of months later, I asked her how about *eternity* — with me, that is. She smiled sweetly and said *yes*. Both of us had come from divorced parents, and being next door to Hollywood where some stars changed partners like some football teams change quarterbacks, we wanted an enduring marriage.

Along about this time Marsha became a Christian. This was my number one prerequisite, that my wife was to be a Christian. Like me, she had been a church member but had never enjoyed a personal relationship with Christ. She'll tell you how this happened in the last chapter of the book.

Bill Bright, the founder of Campus Crusade, and his wife Vonette, lived near the UCLA campus. We spent a lot of time with them. After the school year ended Marsha worked in the Crusade office.

We'll always have a warm spot in our hearts for Bill and Vonette. I guess you could call them our spiritual parents.

Of course they had a lot of other UCLA kids besides us to shepherd. They gave no-one-knows-how-many hours to entertaining and counseling. The Crusade movement kept growing and growing at UCLA and by this time was spreading to other campuses as far away as the East Coast. One reason, I believe, was because of Bill Bright's strategy to win campus leaders who had influence among the student body. For example, who could help but be impressed by Rafer Johnson's witness since everyone at UCLA knew him? Rafer not only was one of the world's greatest athletes (he then held the world record in the decathlon), but he was a campus personality. Rafer had become a Christian through a Youth For Christ Bible Club in high school and after coming to UCLA became active in Campus Crusade. (Though he has retired from athletics, Rafer is still in the news. After Bob Kennedy was shot, Rafer helped capture the man who was later convicted of the Senator's murder.)

Because I lacked half a semester's ROTC training to qualify for an officer's commission in the Army Reserves, I planned to return after the 1957 pro season and finish up during the '58 spring semester. Marsha and I scheduled our wedding for December 28 — give or take a few days, depending upon whether or not the Colts won the title. Winning didn't seem too likely since the new Colts had been in the NFL only four seasons and during that time had won only one-third of their games — 16 of 48.

Both team and fan interest needed building in Baltimore. The Colts had lost their pro franchise in the old All-American Football Conference back in 1950 when only 95,000 fans attended six home games. Carroll Rosenbloom and several other prominent Baltimore citizens rescued the club from oblivion and got the team into the NFL in 1953 by selling 15,000 season tickets within a seven-week period. Mr. Rosenbloom later bought out his partners and now owns 100 per cent of the stock in the club that has multiplied his investment many times over.

The 1953 Colts started with some great guys whom I came to know well in later years. The '53 hosses had defensive tackle Art Donovan, guard Art Spinney, linebacker Bill Pellington, defensive end Gino Marchetti, and back Don Shula. They picked up center Buzz Nutter, offensive end Jim Mutscheller, defensive end Don Joyce, and guard Alex Sandusky in 1954.

With Weeb Ewbank as head coach, the Colts signed up more talent in 1955: Fullback Alan Ameche, end Raymond Berry, center Dick Szymanski, halfback L. G. (Long Gone) Dupre, quarterback George Shaw. The next year John Unitas, Lenny

Moore, and Gene "Big Daddy" Lipscomb moved into the stables and in 1957 Jim Parker, Ordell Braase, Milt Davis, Steve Myhra, Andy Nelson, and I came on.

All during June I was sizing up the Colts, wondering how I would fit into the squad, hoping I could show Weeb Ewbank and his coaching staff something in the upcoming bout between the College All-Stars and last year's NFL champion New York Giants.

What was billed as the greatest array of college graduating football talent ever assembled began practice in early July. I'll list a few: Paul Hornung, Jim Parker, Jon Arnett, John Brodie, Ron Kramer, Len Dawson, Henry Jordan, Earl Leggett, Lamar Lundy, Tommy McDonald, Del Shofner, Paul Wiggin, Abe Woodson, and Jimmy Brown.

I had played with and against some of these guys in the Shrine Bowl. Some, like Jimmy Brown, I was seeing for the first time. Jimmy really appeared to have the stuff. When he made a run, his granite legs pumped like the pistons in a souped-up hot rod.

The Chicago papers ran some stories about my Bible reading. One writer made it appear that all I did was read the Bible and play football. Another took off on Sunday football and quoted me as saying that since farmers milked cows on Sunday, I saw no reason why I couldn't play football. I guess I said that.

Such writing gave background color to a little scrimmage incident between me and Ron Kramer. I must have been playing too rough, because Ron up and smacked me in the mouth. It took 16 stitches to sew my lip together. But I didn't hold a grudge and I don't think Ron did either.

What a game! I think some wise guy weatherman must have tried to turn Lake Michigan upside down and empty it out on Soldiers' Field. The fans took cover, but we had to play in the rain for three quarters.

All-Star Coach Curly Lambeau started me at right linebacker. Two old West Coast foes, John Brodie and Jon Arnett also started. Brodie took us in for a score the first time we got the ball. Then the Giants began pushing us around. They won 22-12. I looked forward to seeing those New Yorkers again.

After the All-Star-Giants game I reported to the Colt training camp in Westminster, Maryland and met the coaches, the veteran players, and the rookies who hoped to make the team.

Parker and I got the most attention because we had been the top draft choices. The way the coaches looked the other newcomers over reminds me of a Yankee baseball story. Whitey Ford let the first four guys get on base, each hitting the first ball pitched to them. Then Casey Stengel came out and asked his catcher, Yogi Berra, "Do you think Whitey has it today?" And Yogi said, "I don't know. I haven't felt one yet." Weeb Ewbank and his staff hadn't "felt" us in action yet.

This was the first of 12 camps I've attended and they've all moved along the same lines. About 30 guys come hoping to make the squad. Most have been drafted and signed to contracts. A few are free agents who come to try out.

Like Yogi Berra, the coaches want to peel out the talent and who has it. They had read scouting reports and looked at films, but the camp and the following pre-season games are the real testing grounds.

Actually a coach can tell a lot about a guy's potential before he puts on the pads. Does he know the rules well? Does he line up correctly? Does he know the overall defense or offense and his position? Does he understand readily what the coach is talking about, or does he have to say, "Wait, Coach, what do you mean?"

The pressure is not only on the newcomers, but on the veterans who didn't do well the previous year and whose jobs are coveted by the new guys. As time moves along, the cutting begins. The head coach will call a guy in and say, "Well, you showed us something, but it's not enough. Thanks for coming." Some will admit, "Coach, you're right. Maybe I'll go back to school."

Some guys sense ahead of time they're going to be cut and don't stay around to hear the verdict. You find their bed empty and their clothes gone in the morning and you know they couldn't stand the embarrassment. A few will report to other clubs and find it tougher there because of the grapevine. An occasional one will latch on to another club. Maybe that coach prefers quickness over speed and the coach who turned him down prefers the opposite.

Training camp isn't altogether a grind. It's a lot of fun getting to know some of the best athletes in the country. I've always liked to be around guys who can teach me something and I've always tried to learn from them.

You find out who are the practical jokesters. At the camp (where I wore a goatee to cover up my stitches) Alex Sandusky killed a ground hog and slipped it in Jim Parker's pants while Jim was asleep. Jim yelled like he had been snake bit. Speaking of snakes, a guy threw a snake into Big Daddy Lipscomb's bed and Big Daddy all but jumped through the ceiling. A more common trick is to put analgesic balm into a guy's shirt. After he has it on underneath his pads and starts sweating, the balm gives him a maddeningly hot feeling. But by then he's on the field and can't take off the pads.

About half of the new candidates are usually mustered out during training camp. The remaining cuts, the most difficult, must be made before the regular season opens to bring the roster down to 40.

But in 1957 the roster limit was 35. This meant more suspense for me, even after I had survived the training camp cuts, during the pre-season games.

Pre-season games show the coach and his assistants what you can do against other pro teams. It separates the college boys who think they have already arrived from those who want to really begin learning what football is all about. Red Grange once said, "College players don't know how to play football. In college you have studies to make up, lectures to attend, scholastic requirements to satisfy. In pro ball you are free from all this. You have nothing to do but eat, drink, and sleep football and that is just what the boys do."

I felt pretty certain I would make the team after I had a taste of the action in the pre-season games. In the second one — against the Chicago Bears in Cincinnati — I picked off two interceptions and we tied the team that had won the 1956 Western Conference Division title in the NFL.

Although I will admit knowing I was a second draft choice

helped. I am sure there have been some fine ball players over-looked by coaches just because of the time element.

I spotted a familiar face on the Bear bench; my old UCLA teammate, Ronnie Knox. After getting out of the National Guard, back in June, Ronnie had signed a three-year contract with the Bears. Ronnie looked happy. I hoped he would make it with the Bears.

After we played the last pre-season game against the Chicago Cardinals the Colt roster dropped to 37 players. Two more had to go to bring the team down to the 35-player limit. Coach Ewbank told me I was definitely on the squad and I felt reas-sured. The newspapers reported four players were on the shaky edge: quarterback Cotton Davidson, linebacker Bill Koman, and two defensive halfbacks, Don Shula and Henry Moore.

The final decision was to release the linebacker Bill Koman and one of the defensive halfbacks, Don Shula. Bill got a job with the Eagles and later with the Cards and stayed in the NFL many more years. Don Shula hooked on with the Wash-ington Redskins where he played a year, before becoming an assistant coach. Cotton Davidson and Henry Moore stayed with us one more year, then Cotton moved to the Dallas Texans.

Coach Ewbank said he could use me as a linebacker and a kicker. I was glad to get these assignments. but I felt badly about Bill Koman losing his job.

With the first regular game of the season in the offing, my fu-ture looked bright. Paul Menton, Sports Editor of the *Baltimore Sun*, said I was the "best prospect" for the Colts' future. He called the squad the "best ever" for Baltimore, but not champions, and projected seven wins and five losses for 1957.

For my Colt training camp I grew a goatee to cover up a little incident in the College All-Star camp between me and Ron Kramer

I'm number 66 and looking where the ball was.

Baltimore's Memorial Stadium. Home of the Colts. Yeah, Team!

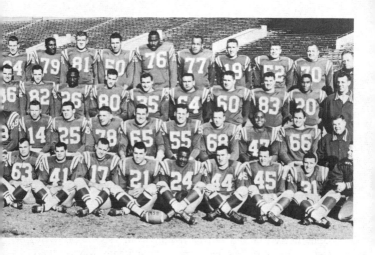

The Baltimore Colts were world football champions in
1958 (above) and 1959 (below). Here are some of the
greatest players to ever touch foot to the gridiron.

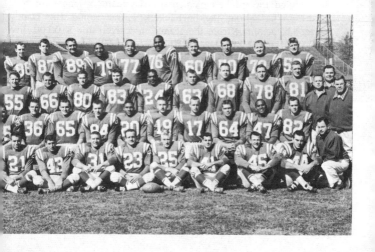

7

"A Change of Life"

With the pre-season games over and the squad pared to the 35-player limit, I anticipated the first league game against the Detroit Lions. Being a team of developing players, the Colts invited a lot of questions. Could Johnny Unitas, the young quarterback who had been signed off the sandlots of Pittsburgh for the price of an 80¢ phone call turn out to be the Cinderella player some predicted? Could ends Jim Mutscheller and Raymond Berry (44 and 37 pass receptions in 1956 respectively) become dangerous deep receivers? Could Lenny Moore, the Colts' 1956 first draft choice, learn to run better after catching the ball? Could Alan Ameche, the All-American from Wisconsin, develop a faster start and get through the holes quicker to prove himself a star fullback? What would the defensive backfield, called the weakest element of the team by some, be able to do? What about the linebackers? And would Big Daddy Lipscomb, acquired from the Rams on waivers for $100.00, live up to his capabilities beside the proven Gino Marchetti, Art Donovan, and Don Joyce in the defensive front four?

Sunday, September 29, finally came. We reported two hours before kickoff for taping. Eddie Block, the trainer, had geared his schedule so each man would be in uniform 45 minutes before game time. Then after warm-ups, we knelt for a short dressing room prayer which I led at the request of Coach Ewbank. I didn't know then that I would be leading pre-game prayers for the next 12 seasons.

Hooray for the Colts! We winged to a 34-14 victory over the Lions. Credit the passing of John Unitas who threw for four touchdowns and the defensive line that held the Lions to a net rushing total of 23 yards. Gino Marchetti and Art Donovan really tied knots in the Lions offense with their bone-cracking tackles. I got in a few licks myself. It was a great thrill to be a starter as a rookie.

Bring on the Bears!

John Unitas showed the ice water in his veins as he took over for injured George Shaw, the starting field general, and led us to a 21-10 win. John threw on fourth down for two touchdowns, one at the Bear eight and another at the Bear nine. Lenny Moore broke through for a 55-yard payoff. The Bears failed to get a single first down by rushing. I made some of the stops and intercepted a late fourth quarter Bear pass to put the game on ice. It was my first league interception.

Bring on the Packers! We were starting to feel like champions. But Weeb Ewbank reminded us we had eleven new men on the squad and ten games to go.

Green Bay lead 10-7 at the half. Then we told the Packers what the "Looney Tunes" cartoon narrator used to say, "That's all, folks." Jim Mutscheller and Alan Ameche each scored three TD's. My second league interception came off Babe Parilli who alternated with the new Packer quarterback from Alabama, Bryan "Bart" Starr. On defense I helped hold the Packers to only 47 yards rushing with Paul Hornung getting 20 yards of that. Old acquaintance Ron Kramer, whom I "vaguely" recalled from the All-Star game in Chicago, hardly got past the line of scrimmage!

What goes up must come down — unless it's outside of the gravity field. The Colts had gone up to the top of the Western Conference. But there's plenty of gravity in the NFL, as we found out the following three weeks.

The Detroit Lions pulled out a 31-27 victory in the closing seconds. It's still so heartbreaking I don't like to talk about it.

Then the Packers came snarling back in the fourth quarter when I thought we had them beat. Babe Parilli heaved a 50-yarder to Bill Howton who outran Henry Moore and put them ahead 24-21.

Coach Ewbank shrugged sadly and said, "We're just seven points from being undefeated."

The next Sunday evening, thanks to the Steelers and their

new quarterback Earl Morrall, we were 13 points from being undefeated.

In the Baltimore gloom I spotted some familiar names in a sports headline about the George Halas-Harvey Knox feud. The story said Papa Knox was mad because Papa Bear hadn't played Ronnie enough for the boy to work up a sweat. Papa Bear said he had suspended Ronnie for "willful violation of the rules and regulations of the club," meaning Ronnie had missed several practices. The report said Papa Knox had called Papa Bear a "skunk" and Papa Bear had labeled Ronnie's Papa a "rabbit." Halas had come back with a final ultimatum. He would give Ronnie a game-to-game contract, whereby he could be released at any time, but only if Papa Harvey Knox would get out of Chicago and stop making public statements concerning Ronnie and the Bears to the press.

I figured this would be the end of Ronnie's football career and so far as I know it was. It's really too bad, for Ronnie might have developed into a great pro player. He was one of the best college passers I have seen in my football career.

But I had to get back to football. You don't win games by discussing the problems of players on other teams.

We were due for a win when we sneaked by the Washington Redskins in a thriller. Messrs. Unitas and Berry teamed up for 224 yards and two scores. Raymond played the greatest game of his career (up to that time) and put his name in the NFL record book by catching 12 passes in a single game. It couldn't have happened to a nicer guy, the hardest worker on the squad. Most of these passes were caught against Don Shula. Shula says, "That's why I went into coaching."

Time and again I had seen Raymond and Johnny practicing pass patterns. Raymond (he prefers this to Ray) would run a route full speed, make a fake or two, and John would throw. Even when John wasn't around, Raymond was almost saying, "Throw me one." All of this throwing could have in his later years caused some of John's arm trouble.

At SMU, Raymond had never been pegged as much of a pro prospect. He played very little until his senior year when he did well in defense and was co-captain of the Mustangs. When he came to the Colts, Weeb Ewbank watched him work out and put him to catching passes.

There was another guy who didn't do too badly in that Washington game — modest Don Shinnick. I recovered the fumble from Eddie LeBaron, the great little Washington quarterback, that set up the winning touchdown.

A Colt defensive player starred in our next game, a 24-14 win over the Chicago Bears — not me this time, but another UCLA alumnus. Milt Davis scored once on a 71-yard return following an interception and ran a second interception 74 yards to the Bear 8. I enjoyed saying to people after the game, "Hey, Milt Davis and I attended the same school." Actually, Milt had graduated in 1954 after being an All-American defensive back, spent two years in the Army and played a couple of games with Detroit before coming to Baltimore as a free agent.

The 49'ers came to town just before Thanksgiving and we took them 27-21 for our sixth victory of the season, the most ever in our NFL history. Yelberton A. Tittle, a former Colt player, called the signals for the men from 'Frisco. Y. A. had more hair then than he has today, but I think he lost some in that game. His gold dust boys had a 21-20 lead in the fourth quarter when Unitas cranked up his arm and passed the Colts to final victory. This put us at the top of the Western Conference Division with a 6-3 record.

Then to make life even more sweet, Marsha came to visit me. She figured the visit might cut down on my phone bill which had been high enough to boost the stock of AT&T. I gave her a mink stole when she arrived. "Most girls get the ring first and the mink later," I had told her. "We'll be different," But she sweet-talked me into buying her an engagement ring, too.

"Honey," I said, "the Colts have been doing real well this year."

She sighed and said, "Yes, and I know why!"

Being a modest fellow, I didn't press her to explain. I merely added, "We have a good chance for the championship and that means —"

"— don't set a date for our wedding," she completed.

"No date," I said, "but be ready just in case."

Marsha stayed to see us beat the Rams 31-14 before the first sellout crowd in Baltimore history. Then the team left for the West Coast where the Colts had dates with the 49'ers and Rams.

Moan! The Old Master's gold dust boys put us through their sluice box and came out four points ahead. Y. A. must have wanted his hair back.

With the one game remaining against the Rams we still had title hopes. A win would give us a tie for the division title with San Francisco and/or Detroit, with the play-off coming in the East.

Marsha and I decided if this happened we would have a quickie wedding Sunday night, December 15, right after the game. If we lost (unthinkable!), I would go back to Baltimore with the team, pack, and return for a planned and proper ceremony, but still not a big wedding. This may have been the only time in history that the date for a wedding hinged on the final outcome of a professional football game.

What happened? A certain stubborn Dutchman named Van Brocklin held it against us for beating his team two weeks before. While the sky pelted the field and stadium with rain, he pelted us with passes. Four went for touchdowns. Final score: 37-21, Rams.

Detroit and San Francisco both won and tied for the division title. Detroit later defeated the 49'ers in the play-off by four points — the same margin the 49'ers had beaten us by two weeks before. Then the Lions moved on to wallop the Eastern Conference Division champion Cleveland Browns 59-14 for the world title. We wound up in third place, the best the Colts had ever done in the NFL, but not enough to take away the sting of missing the championship.

It was a long flight back to Baltimore after the Ram defeat. Marsha had actually packed her clothes and had her wedding suit in the car during the December 15th game. But because of the loss we decided to wait until after Christmas.

As we flew along above the clouds, I looked at my dispirited teammates. Some were sleeping or playing cards. Some were grousing about the defeat and replaying the game. *They're a great bunch of guys,* I thought, *but I'd rather have Marsha's company tonight.*

Several hundred die-hard Colt fans met us at the airport. They cheered and called for us to go all the way in '58. At the moment I wasn't thinking much about football. I just wanted to pack and get back on the road to California.

Milt Davis, who tied with two other guys for most NFL pass interceptions (10) during the past season, and I went together. Milt, a Negro, is one of the nicest guys I've ever met. But wouldn't you know that some crummy restaurants in Oklahoma and Texas wouldn't serve us at tables? I grumbled more about it than Milt. We ate in the car. We've come a long way in race relations in this country, but not far enough. Milt is now a big wheel in the Los Angeles school system.

By Christmas Day we were in Los Angeles. I got my best present the next day when Marsha and I were married. "This way," I told friends, "I can get by with one present for Christmas and our anniversary." (It hasn't worked out that way though.) The crowd included sportswriter Sam Ponton who wrote a rather unorthodox description of the wedding for his newspaper. Sam missed a few details, which Marsha says are not minor, but I like what he said.

"Appearing before a small group of select friends, in a white ensemble with blue trim and a beautiful white orchid corsage, 'How's that for a start?' Marsha Tatlow became the bride of Don Shinnick in ceremonies at the First Baptist Church in Burbank.

"Miss Tatlow's dress, . . . was white trimmed in blue. I don't know just what kind of collar or sleeves it had, could be Queen Anne collar and the sleeves could have been tapering. There could have been something old, borrowed and blue but I didn't see that either.

"Miss Bonnie Tatlow, the bride's sister served as bridesmaid and was gowned, also in a white, very pretty dress with blue accessories. Can't tell you about the flowers because I don't know anything about them.

"Don's brother served as best man and seating of the guests was ably handled by the bridesmaid's boy friend.

"The organist played some tunes, real good too. A vocalist sang some love songs, one of them was 'Oh Promise Me' and the ceremonies began.

"Down the aisle came the bride, bridesmaid and father, Denny Tatlow. By the way Father Denny was shaking you would have thought he was getting married.

"The bride and groom finally said their 'I do's' and they are now wife and husband.

"A line formed on each side at the walk leading from the church and everyone was armed with a handfull of rice. But Don was calling the signals and he and Marsha came charging out of the vestibule, each with a whole box full. At the end of this scrimmage, there was enough white stuff lying around to call it a 'White Day After Christmas.'

"The newly married pair will spend their honeymoon someplace up the West Coast line. That's all the information we could get. But when asked the usual question about tonight and tomorrow, Don did say he was going to watch the late-late movie and get in a round of golf the next morning.

"The bride and groom's mothers were both attired in very pretty clothes and looked young enough to be brides themselves.

"The Shinnicks will make their home in Los Angeles and Don will graduate from UCLA in the spring."

After our honeymoon (during which I didn't even think of golf) I completed my final semester at UCLA while Marsha worked in the Campus Crusade office. Plenty of speaking requests came in from Youth for Christ, Campus Crusade, and other groups. I took as many as I could handle, giving first preference to those who asked me first. I talked some about football, but always about Christ whether I was addressing a Jewish Men's Club or a Baptist Sunday school banquet. I introduced myself to the Jewish group as a "Christian layman," then said, "One of my best college friends was Jewish, my head trainer with the Colts is Jewish, and the owner of the Colts is Jewish. You can see I can't afford to be prejudiced. I don't mean to force my beliefs on anyone, but I do want to share with you what I know about the greatest Jew who ever lived, my Saviour Jesus Christ."

The numerous invitations to speak encouraged me to believe

that I could witness for Christ as a pro football player to people who might otherwise not hear the Gospel. This alone was cause enough to ignore the question of Sunday ball which some church people continue to raise. One time I threw the question back at a minister. "Why do you work on Sunday?" He said, "Because I'm called by God." I said, "That's exactly why I play football on Sunday."

8

"1958 — That Wonderful Year!"

That's what my confident bride titled her first scrapbook about me.

It was old folks at home in the training camp. Just about everyone from the 1957 squad was back. The '57 All-Pros, Art Donovan, Gino Marchetti, John Unitas, and Milt Davis, were anxious to repeat. Unitas had been voted "Most Valuable Player" in 1957 for completing 172 of 301 passes for a league-leading 2,550 yards and 24 touchdowns. Milt Davis had performed a rare feat by winning "All-Pro" during his first year. And those twin terrors, Art and Gino, had become the "most feared" pass rushers by opposing quarterbacks. Art's fighting instinct may have come from his father, the famed boxing referee who had worked more title fights than any other man.

Fast man Lenny Moore, the League's top touchdown tallier in 1957, was chafin' at the bit to make more TD runs. Alan "the Horse" Ameche, who had been the Colts' leading ground-gainer during the past three years, felt the same way. Raymond Berry, the second best pass receiver in the NFL in 1957, seemed on the edge of greatness. Jim Mutscheller, who had snagged eight touchdown passes in 1957, was anxious to complement Berry from his tight end position. The rest of us were just as anxious as the stand-outs to bring a championship to Baltimore.

But the pre-season activity didn't indicate that we could turn the trick. Or so the sportswriters prophesied. They pointed to our exhibition losses. Perhaps they didn't consider Weeb Ewbank's strategy of playing rookies to get a good look at them. Or the desire of a young, hungry team. Or the fan spirit stirred up by Carroll Rosenbloom in Baltimore, which is so vital to a team's morale. Where else but in Baltimore would every seat be filled for an inter-squad game?

Me — I planned on doing better than the year before. This time as the middle linebacker. When the final trimming was done, I was back in the starting lineup again and eager to put the hoofs to the 1957 NFL Champion Lions in the season opener.

A win over the 1957 NFL title winner would give us a psychological boost at the beginning of the season. The Lions had captured Western Conference honors four times during the past six years and in the 1957 title game had made hamburger out of the Cleveland Browns defense. With Texans Bobby Layne and Tobin Rote alternating at quarterback, fullback John Henry Johnson, and All-pro linebacker Joe Schmidt, the Lions looked ferocious.

But my buddies and I in the Colt defense turned them into tame house cats for the first 13 minutes of the game. They didn't get a single first down while our offense went ahead 7-0 on a Lenny Moore run. Then they suddenly turned back into beasts and roared ahead 15-14 early in the fourth quarter.

We moaned twice when Lion linebacker Bob Long (an old UCLA teammate of mine) grabbed a pass from Unitas, ran it back to the Colt 10, then fumbled, with Alex Karras retaining the ball for the Lions. But our defense turned the Lions back into house cats. They even missed a field goal attempt on fourth down. After we took over on our 20, John Henry Johnson hit the Colts' Bill Pellington in an argument, and the penalty gave us more yardage. The fans began chanting, "Take us in, John," and Unitas did, ringing up our twentieth point on a pass to Berry.

Then after we got the ball back, Unitas faked to Ameche and handed off to "Long Gone" Dupre who put the touchdown icing on the cake for a 28-15 win.

It was a sweet victory over the team that had beaten us the year before by scoring two touchdowns in the last 75 seconds of play.

Next came the Bears, who hadn't been defeated in their last seven starts. Papa Bear George Halas had said weeks before that his team would be gunning for the Colts this year, because

Baltimore was then the only team in the Western Conference holding a winning record over the Bears. For that matter the Bears were the only team against which the Colts showed a winning record, period!

We didn't intend to be chewed up by the hungry Bears. During the week before the game placards with numbers appeared all over our locker room walls. The linebackers — Bill Pellington, Leo Sanford, and I — had No. 28 — Willie Galimore in front of our lockers. Art Donovan and Big Daddy Lipscomb looked at No. 35 — Rick Casares. Jim Parker, who didn't need to be reminded, glowered at Doug Atkins' number.

What a game! The Colt offense galloped all over the field, churning up 51 points. We scored 27 points in the first quarter. Lenny Lyles, a rookie from the University of Louisville (also known as John Unitas University), took a Bear kick-off 3 yards behind the goal line and ran the 103 yards for a touchdown in a reported 10 seconds flat! The Bear offense took a few pounds of our flesh, but didn't quite score enough points — 38. We literally dragged ourselves off the field and through the tunnel and into the dressing room. Came a voice, "How 'bout the prayer?" The grunting and gear slapping stopped. We knelt. Time seemed to stand still as I led them in the Lord's prayer.

Gino Marchetti, looking as if he had been plucked out of a threshing machine, stepped out and said to the Colt owner, "The team wants you to have the ball this time."

Mr. Rosenbloom was too touched to make a speech. All he managed was, "Thanks, gang."

It had been a great team victory.

Two down and ten to go. Green Bay came next.

On defense we linebackers tried a strategy we had used against the Bears. We played close to the line, figuring we could always drop back to cover on pass defense. Bart Starr, who sometimes seems to have brains clear down into his shoulder pads, realized what we were doing. He threw behind us and we woke up at half-time on the short end of a 17-7 score. We wouldn't have had that one touchdown if defensive halfback Andy Nelson, a second year man from Memphis State, hadn't intercepted one of Bart's aerials.

Coach Ewbank gave us a little talk and we restyled our defense. You may have wondered why a team so often will play completely different ball in the second half. The reason is that it sometimes takes thirty minutes of football to size up the opponent.

We came back and John Unitas connected with Mutscheller for another score. Then I gobbled up one of Bart's beauties to set the Colts up for a field goal by Steve Myhra which knotted the score at 17-17.

Andy Nelson grabbed off his second interception and ran it back 52 yards for a go-ahead touchdown — his first in the pros.

Battling Bart wouldn't quit. With 46 seconds to go, he threw to Hornung. I had my eye on pretty boy Paul who had just come on the field. I swiped the ball from under his nose and that was the game.

We ran into the dressing room where someone had a case of pop ready for a celebration. (Honest! The Colts celebrate with pop because it's healthier and there's also a little ole NFL rule forbidding alcohol.) Then after our customary prayer, Don Joyce hollered, "We just stuck our hands in the red hot coals and pulled them out."

To which someone replied, "Yeah, but we've still got the scars."

Hero Nelson didn't talk about his game-saving interceptions. "I could have been the goat of the game," he said gratefully. We knew he was referring to a freak play in the first quarter when he had used one hand to try and intercept a pass that would have otherwise probably fallen incomplete. The pass rolled down his arm, over his shoulder, and into the arms of the Packers' Don McIlhenny who scored. But none of us were scolding him for that. We were all thinking of the win that put us at the top of the Western Conference. And we were thinking that we had won the first three last year and lost the next three. We hoped history wouldn't repeat itself.

It didn't. The next week we made it four in a row with an easy 40-14 win over the Lions. It was the first time the Colts had defeated Detroit at home.

The Redskins were next. We had a couple of things going against them. First, they had taken us to the cleaners 27-7 in a pre-season game where we had made a pile of mistakes. Second, George Marshall, owner of the 'Skins, had said something uncomplimentary about our center, Buzz Nutter. We felt that Buzz, a drawling West Virginian and an ex-'Skin didn't deserve Mr. Marshall's remarks.

We were out to win the game for Buzz.

In the opening minutes the 'Skins all but walked to an easy score, that shocked our home fans. But we shifted our defense to their strong side — the "hamburger side," we called it. They never crossed the goal line again. Everyone blocked. We batted down passes. Lenny Lyles ran one kickoff back for 101 yards. Gentleman Eddie LeBaron earned only 16 net yards in 16 pass attempts and got knocked down more than a few times. Eddie, 5'7" and only 165 pounds, is one of the nicest, nerviest, smallest, and toughest guys I ever played against. When knocked down, he would usually say, "What? You again?" In 1957 he had been the number two passer in the league with 99 completions out of 167 attempts. But we couldn't let even a gentleman like Eddie beat us. We won 35-10.

We now had five wins in a row, with the Bears only one game behind in the Western Conference and snapping at our heels. Our defense had given up only 94 points to date; only the Giants had done better by giving up 77 points.

Poor Packers. We beat them so badly, I'm ashamed to mention the score. But I might as well since you can find it in the record: 56-0. I'm going to be charitable and not mention the details, except to say that it was the worst defeat suffered by any team during the season.

But the defeat hurt us in the most vulnerable place. John Unitas was kneed in the chest and suffered a fractured rib and a punctured lung.

Next came the Giants — and with Unitas out, Charlie Conerly and company (Frank Gifford, Kyle Rote, Alex Webster, Sam Huff, etc.) lived up to their names. The Giants then had two great future coaches in assistants Tom Landry (defense) and Vince Lombardi (offense).

The Giants had operated since 1925 and had qualified for ten world championship games — more than any other NFL member.

The Colts were the infants of the NFL, having been admitted prematurely in 1950, thrown out in 1951-52, then readmitted in 1953 after fan interest picked up.

George Shaw, our backup quarterback, took charge in place of Unitas who was recuperating from the injured lung. George put us ahead 14-7 on two touchdown passes in the first half. Then the Giants took the lead on a Conerly-Rote pass and a 13-yard run by Frank "do-everything" Gifford.

The fourth quarter turned into a cardiac finish. We came back to tie on Shaw's pass to Lenny Moore, then a few minutes later Sam Huff intercepted and the Giants moved into position for the winning field goal by Pat Summerall. The game ended 24-21 in favor of the New Yorkers with us itching for a rematch.

Though it was our first loss of the year, we remained in first place in the Western Conference. "Can't win 'em all," one of the guys said in resignation.

"Yeah," I replied, "but I sure hope we play the Giants again — for the world championship." Such a prospect wasn't unlikely because the Giants were then only a game back of the Cleveland Browns in the Eastern Conference race.

But we all knew that first we had to win our Conference to qualify for the championship game. We still had five games to go — one against the Bears and two each against the Rams and the 49'ers.

We took the Bears 17-0 to stay all alone at the top in the Western Conference. This marked the first time the Bears had been shut out in 12 years and 148 games.

The Rams fell to us next in a game that was closer than the 34-7 score indicated. We went into the fourth quarter ahead 13-7 and behind in total yardage gained. Fast-finish Unitas coolly took us in for three quick scores and that was all for the men from LA.

Now if we could beat the 49'ers and Pittsburgh could cage the Bears for us, we would clinch the Conference title. It was something to look forward to the next Sunday.

We wanted that win awfully bad — maybe so bad that we were tensed up the first half. We fumbled, missed tackles, and looked like cellar-dwellers instead of the Conference leaders.

Y.A. Tittle and his boys were charitable until the last five minutes of the half when they added three more touchdowns to the one they scored during the first five minutes. The half ended with us behind 27-0. The 49'ers had missed one conversion try.

Because of the time zone differential we knew Pittsburgh had beaten the Bears. Now all we had to do was win. Weeb Ewbank wrote on the chalkboard: "4 TD's." "That's what you've got to get," he said crisply. "And you can't let them score either."

Fourteen plays later Ameche went over from the one for our first. Unitas uncorked a 50-yard pass to Mutscheller for the second. Carl Taseff intercepted and set the stage for a Unitas scoring pass to Berry for the third. Lenny Moore, whom we had recently nicknamed "Sputnik," took off like a zig-zagging rocket and ran an incredible 73 yards for the fourth. The conversion put us a point ahead, 28-27. A little later Steve Myhra kicked a field goal for the final tally. Steve, an alumnus of the University of North Dakota, had never seen a pro football game until coming to Baltimore in 1957.

We ran to the locker room and knelt in prayer. "Heavenly Father, we praise Thy name and thank Thee for everything, including this win and Your protection," I said. Then we recited the Lord's prayer together.

I looked around and saw Art Donovan and Art Spinney crying. (They weren't the only ones.) The two had been roommates and teammates at Boston College. They had come to the Colts in 1950 and played on the team that was voted out of the NFL because of lack of financial support and fan enthusiasm. They played on the short end of such scores as 70-21, 70-28, and 55-13. Now they were Western Conference champions along with the rest of us.

We had clinched the title with two games yet to go. We lost both to the Rams and the 49'ers. I have no explanation. Call it a letdown if you wish. But the Rams won by only two points and the 49'ers by only nine. The Bears won their last two games and wound up second in the Western Conference, one game behind us.

The Giants beat the Browns 13-10 in their last game of the season to force the Browns into a play-off game the following

Sunday. We watched the game, sort of hoping the Giants would win. They had beaten us by three earlier in the year and we wanted a second whack at them. The Giants won 10-0, giving Cleveland three defeats for the season, all to the Giants.

This set the stage for the 1958 world title game — the contest that people still call the greatest football game ever played.

9

"The Greatest Football Game Ever Played"

People who are not even Baltimore Colt fans are still calling it that. I know I've never played in a greater game — if you measure greatness by fan interest, exciting plays, suspense, comebacks, and what's at stake.

Baltimore hadn't had a major sports championship since the old Orioles won the National League Pennant way back in 1896. The World Series hadn't started then. The ill-born Colts had never even come close in their few years of pro football competition.

But this had to be the year. We had to beat the New York Giants in Yankee Stadium on the same ground where Babe Ruth had put his home town of Baltimore on the sports map.

The Giants had beaten us by three points back on November 9. Charlie Conerly, the Giants 37-year-old quarterback, had said after that game, "We out-gutted them" — a remark we didn't forget. The quote with its source stayed before us in big letters on our bulletin board the entire week before the game.

Sixteen thousand rabid Colt fans jammed into New York for the game. In subways, buses, hotel lobbies, and all over town, you could hear the familiar, "Gimme a C! Gimme an O! Gimme an L! Gimme a T! Gimme an S! Yeah, Colts!"

Over 70,000 jammed every inch of space in Yankee Stadium. Fifty million watched the game on NBC television — the biggest audience to date to watch a football game.

Before the game Weeb Ewbank received a 20-foot-long telegram signed by 800 supporters in his home town of Richmond, Indiana. Each had paid a quarter to send the message wishing us victory with the list of names.

We flew into New York on December 28, two days after our first wedding anniversary for a day's rest and preparation. As the countdown proceeded, the tenseness grew. A few laughs helped us loosen up. Big Daddy Lipscomb came down the hall to the taping room singing, "Tell Me That You Love Me." Jim Parker plopped his 272 pounds on a frame chair and collapsed in a heap. Fortunately only his dignity was hurt.

When we left the bus at the Stadium, a fireman hollered to Art Donovan, "Hey, Donovan, I hope this team is better than the one you played on at Mt. St. Michael's." Art laughed. He had already told us that his old neighborhood was a few blocks away. He remembered people joshing him at the local candy store about always being on the losing team. Art admitted that until this year he had never been on a winning team — not even in grade school!

We arrived at the Stadium a little after 12:30 and began dressing slowly. There was plenty of time before the opening kick-off at 2:05. Unitas and some of the guys began throwing the ball around. Alan Ameche recited part of the Gettysburg address. Don't ask me why. I sat off by myself wanting to get my mind in order. A Baltimore writer asked about my feelings and I said, "I think we're ready."

Weeb Ewbank called us together. He went down the roster and noted all the players who had been dropped by other teams — 14 out of the 35. Six had come to us as trades, seven as free agents, and "Daddy" Lipscomb for the $100.00 waiver price. Bill Pellington had been sent away by the Cleveland Browns after only one try in scrimmage. He had then hitchhiked to the Colts' training camp from his home in New Jersey. We had been called, as Weeb pointed out in his before-game talk, a bunch of rejects, retreads, and new recruits. He really got the team pride up in that talk.

At 1:50 I asked the guys for a few seconds of meditation, then I led them in the Lord's prayer.

A few minutes later we trotted onto the field. Only two days before New Year's, the weather was springlike. It was as if the weatherman had become confused and thought the Yankees were opening the baseball season. But the confetti thrown by fans made it seem like a snowstorm in brilliant sunlight.

The Colts kicked off and the game was under way. As I moved into the middle linebacker's slot, I thought of all the people cheering us on — not the least, Marsha and the other Colt wives who were home watching on television.

If you're a Colt or Giant football fan, you probably saw the game — or certainly you've read about it, perhaps a dozen times. It was certainly no game for a heart patient or for a coach with ulcers. There were more heart-stopping thrills than points on the scoreboard, and more heroes than stripes across the field. "This was the super colossal game of them all," said NFL Commissioner Bert Bell, a man not known for rash enthusiasm.

Actually the first half was not unusually thrilling. The Giants who had worked so hard to get into the title game looked as if they couldn't care less about winning.

The New Yorkers made their first big mistake in pegging Lenny Moore as the most dangerous receiver and assigning two men to him after Unitas threw a long pass to Lenny. Cool John took note and made Raymond Berry his primary receiver. The Giants frequently covered him with only one man. This may have been the most fateful decision of the game.

We made a mistake in the first quarter which we quickly corrected. The Giants blocked a Colt field goal when guard Art Spinney turned out instead of in, giving the Giants' great linebacker Sam Huff a clear route to block the kick. Art corrected himself and did the reverse on the next Colt field goal try.

All the Giants could manage in the first quarter was a three-point field goal. The Colts earned two touchdowns, the first on a two-yard plunge by Alan "the Horse" Ameche and the second on a Unitas to Berry pass from the 15 as time in the first half was running out. Before this play, Unitas had completed only two passes to Raymond in the game.

There were at least five incidents in the first half where the Giants goofed.

They lost the ball three times on fumbles, two by Frank Gifford who had a reputation for sure-handedness. Of course this might have been caused by the special new defense Artie,

Big Daddy and myself put on Gifford — at the suggestion of defensive coach John Bridgers.

A fourth incident came when Colt halfback Milt Davis bumped Gifford off balance, probably preventing Frank from extending his 38-yard run to the end zone. The fifth came when Giant halfback Alex Webster got into the clear deep in Colt territory, but slipped and missed an almost certain pass reception and touchdown.

We were confident but not jubilant during the half time break. Weeb Ewbank told us we had to keep ahead and not take anything for granted.

I don't know what Coach Jim Lee Howell told the Giants, but they lived up to their names in the second half — except I didn't like what Sam Huff did to Raymond Berry. On the fourth play following the kickoff, Berry caught a Unitas pass. Huff tackled him right near our bench and put the knee to him. I lost my cool and jumped on Huff from the bench. The guys pulled me off and the game went on.

The Giants got the ball back on downs and our defense went in to show 'em what we thought of the way Huff had treated Berry. The Giants lost eight yards in three downs and had to punt. Then Unitas took the Colts to the Giant three and a first down.

Whoa! The Giants put the skids on Ameche. He tried three times and Unitas tried once, but they couldn't get over. If the Giants hadn't held right there when we were leading 14-3 I think the rest of the game would have been a rout. But by holding, they served notice they intended to fight to the dying gasp.

That goal line stand really fired up the Giants when they took over. Conerly moved them eight yards in two plays to safer ground. Then he fired off a 62-yard pass to Kyle Rote at our 25. Andy Nelson hit Rote, causing him to drop the ball and in the melee Alex Webster picked up the ball and carried it to our one before being knocked out of bounds. Melvin Triplett plunged for the touchdown and Pat Summerall converted. The Giant fans roared loud enough to be heard back in Baltimore. Colts 14 — Giants 10.

Less than three minutes later, the aroused Giants scored again, this time on a Conerly pass to Gifford. Milt Davis rode Gifford's back across the goal line. (Milt was the only player on the field wearing tennis shoes. His injured foot had been shot full of novocain.) Summerall converted. Giants 17 — Colts 14.

The fourth quarter was brutal. It was like one long meat grinder as both teams clawed and fought for the ball. Gino Marchetti had his ankle broken in two places and had to be carried off the field. Once after a Giant fumble, Unitas threw long to Lenny Moore. It was complete at the goal but ruled out of bounds. The crowd noise of the Giant fans probably shook the Empire State Building. The Colt fans must have chewed off a thousand fingernails.

The Giants got the ball back on downs, then punted to the Colt 14. With 1:56 remaining, the Giant fans were winding up for the victory roar. But they didn't know John Unitas, the coolest thing this side of the North Pole.

Twice John threw incomplete and twice the Giant fans roared.

On third he connected for 11 yards to Lenny Moore. First down. Another incompletion. Another crowd roar. The Giants were double-teaming Lenny. Look out! One, two, three — all completed passes to Raymond Berry, moving the ball from the 25 to the Giant 13. They were the three most important receptions ever made by an offensive end.

Now the Giant fans were chewing their fingernails.

Seven seconds showed on the scoreboard clock.

Without huddling the Colts went for the tying field goal. It was the 13th play since the Colts had last taken possession.

Steve Myhra wore a big cast to protect his broken left wrist. But his foot was okay and he put it over. Score: 17-17.

Pandemonium!

Although the Colts kicked and the Giants got off one more play, very few noticed. Everyone was waiting for the sudden-death overtime.

In the brief time-out, we got the word from Weeb Ewbank: "Win it for Gino."

The referees flipped a half dollar to see who would get the ball first. John Unitas called tails. The coin landed head up.

We had to kick off to the Giants. Then we had to get the ball before they could move into field goal range. The simple rule of sudden death was that the team first scored on was dead. And after having coming this far, we weren't ready to have our coffin lid nailed down.

The Giants' Don Maynard took the kick on his ten, fumbled (gigantic crowd gasp), but recovered and carried to the twenty. Frank Gifford made four yards. Conerly faked a draw play, pulling me and Bill Pellington in, then tossed the ball toward Bob Schnelker who dove in vain for the ball. On third and six Conerly danced back, looking for a receiver. He saw no one open and tried to run hard outside our left end. My linebacking partner Bill Pellington slowed him as he slammed toward a first down. I came in from the side, twisting my body sidewise, and stopped his forward momentum *one foot* from a first down.

It was the biggest tackle assist I ever made. Had I been a split second later, the Giants would have had a fresh series of downs.

The Giants decided to play it safe and kick.

The Colts took the Giants punt on their twenty and "Long Gone" Dupre made eleven yards on the first play. Three more plays and another first down on the Colts 41. Then on the next series, Unitas was thrown for a loss. Third and fifteen. Unitas called for a pass to the right to Lenny, but Lenny was covered. The Giants' Andy Robustelli roared toward John, but Jim Parker bottled him up. Suddenly Unitas saw that Carl Karilivacz, covering Berry, had slipped. He waved Berry deep, threw, and Raymond gobbled it in at the Giants 43. First down!

And then . . . catastrophe! Not for the Colts, but for the TV watchers which included Marsha and most of the Colt wives in Baltimore. It was worse than NBC's famous switch to *Heidi* in 1968 at the expense of the closing minute of a New York Jet victory. It was NBC this time (CBS later got the NFL TV rights). The network explained later that overenthusiastic fans at the Stadium, pressing for a better view of the sudden-death action, disconnected the cable that brought power into the network's equipment room.

While the TV watchers were diving for their radios, Unitas

fooled the Giants (they were looking for a pass) and handed off
to Ameche who ran for 23 big yards. First down for the Colts
on the Giant 20!

At this point Unitas could have called on Myhra for another
field goal which would have been enough to win. If the kick
was blocked, the offensive line would be blamed. If Myhra
missed, it would be his fault. John chose to go for the touchdown, where if he lost the ball — and the game — the blame
would be his.

Dupre saw nothing but Giants on the first down; on second
down Unitas passed to Berry, complete for a first down on the
Giants eight.

The television came back on for the folks at home.

The Giants limited Ameche to a one-yard gain. Second and
goal at the seven.

Now Unitas caught the Giants off-balance with a pass they
hadn't anticipated and which if they had intercepted might have
spelled sudden death for the Colts. He lofted the ball over
Cliff Livingston to Jim Mutscheller who was brought down on
the one.

Unitas called to Referee Ron Gibbs, "If we try a field goal on
the third down and miss, do we get another kick on the fourth?"

Gibbs shook his head. "Sudden death is just like regulation
time. One kick is all."

The Colts lined up. Unitas handed off to Ameche who pounded
for the goal line. Powerhouse blocks by Mutscheller and Moore
opened up a hole and Ameche squirted through.

It was the thirteenth play for the Colts in the sudden death
overtime. Later someone remembered that Myhra had kicked
the tying field goal in the thirteenth play. And that this was
the thirteenth game for the Colts in 1958. Was 13 our lucky
number?

Final score: Colts 23 — Giants 17.

Why didn't the Colts try for the conversion to make it 24?
Are you kidding! After the official signalled the winning touch-
down, the goal posts were down before you could say John
Unitas.

What a finish! For one of the few times in my life I was at a loss for words. But Art Donovan expressed the way we all felt. "We out-gutted them," he said with relish.

Gino Marchetti was, according to the Colts' team physician, "probably the happiest man who ever broke his ankle."

Raymond Berry was his usual quiet self, even after someone told him he had set a record for the most passes (12 for 178 yards) caught in a title game. Unitas had set a record for most yards gained on passes (349) in a title game. The losing Giants had set a record for most fumbles (6) in a championship game.

Regarding Berry, someone noted to Giant owner Jack Mara that he wore contact lenses and could hardly see. "Sure," Mara said grimly, "he can't see anything but footballs."

We prayed and dressed. Then it was up, up, and away to Baltimore.

Thirty-thousand people were waiting for us at the airport. The pilot landed away from the crowd, but the crowd saw the plane. By the time they got us into a bus, there were more fans on top of the bus than Colts inside. A Baltimore TV announcer was trapped and had to cut his mike cord to get away. People fainted. Women's shoes were all over the place. The bus driver ran over one women's foot. Some of the guys had their cars at the airport, but had to ride the bus into town and come back for them after the crowd left.

It was a mad, mad, wonderful evening.

Only the Giants, their fans, and some bettors were mad because Giant backers refused to pay off on the grounds that a sudden death overtime had never been played before.

Actually one had. The Giants and the Rams had played a sudden death in an exhibition game back in 1955.

The score of that game: Rams 23 — Giants 17.

One more interesting coincidence.

John Unitas, No. 19, received a new Corvette from *Sport* magazine, for being named the title game's most outstanding player. Bob Turley, the Yankee pitcher who lived in a Baltimore suburb, had already won a Corvette from *Sport* for being the "most outstanding player" in the 1958 World Series. His number: 19, of course.

10

"Two for Two"

The first week in January, I felt like that line used by Ultra Brite toothpaste: after the sudden death title game with the Giants, everything else was just football.

Maybe that's because I wasn't named All-Pro and given a trip to the pro bowl. Unitas, Ameche, Moore, Berry, Parker, Marchetti, Joyce, and Lipscomb all made the All-League team. There were so many Colts on the Western Conference squad that they should have called it the Baltimore Derby. But how could they have overlooked No. 66, the Colts' great middle linebacker?

Anyway, the excitement finally died down and we began talking about something else beside the greatest game ever played. I went away for six months of training to fulfill my Army commitment. I was a big shot second lieutenant and a platoon leader. But no one seemed particularly impressed about my accomplishments on the football field. I began to think that either I didn't look like a football player or no one had ever heard of Don Shinnick!

I studied biological and radiological warfare. (Hmmmmmm, maybe that's what the Philadelphia Eagles need to teach their players.) Marsha and I lived in Army housing at Fort Benning, Georgia, and I had several weekend speaking engagements in the Southeastern part of the country. Then I went out to "Fort Ord" to finish my Army tour.

It got to be that time again — the start of another season. We won four and lost two of our pre-season games, including a win over the College All-Stars. The oddsmakers favored us and the Giants to repeat as champs of our respective divisions and meet again for the title. We had about the same defensive and offensive lineups as in '58. For example, John Unitas had his same "palace guards": Buzz Nutter, Art Spinney, Alex Sandusky, Jim Parker, and George Preas. The slogan "Unitas We Stand" had become a permanent fixture in Baltimore, although some worried about what might happen if Unitas should get a crippling injury. They also wondered if rookies Jerry Richardson and Dave Shearer could fill the shoes of offensive ends Berry and Mutscheller, if they should be injured.

The defense looked good with the familiar front four: Joyce and Marchetti, Donovan and "Big Daddy." Weeb Ewbank said he was set at linebacking with Pellington, Szymanski, and Shinnick. (I returned to right linebacker.) The Colts had a good defensive backfield, too, with Ray Brown or John Sample, Milt Davis, Andy Nelson, and Carl Taseff.

However, Buddy Young, the former Colt and Baltimore disc jockey, said that the greatest thing we had going for us was the fan in the stand. Of course you can't win with just fans, but then and now the Colts have thousands of fantastic, fanatical rooters. When the Colt named Dixie pranced around the field after each touchdown, when the Colt Corralls (members wear 10-gallon blue hats and monogrammed shirts) yelled, "Gimme a C . . .", when the Colts get the ball and 50,000 voices screamed, "Take us in, John" —well, you had to be a sphinx in uniform for the spirit not to get to you. Now the fans would really have cheered if they had known their favorite linebacker was going to be a papa!

The Lions tried to do us in in front of our opening day crowd in Baltimore. They had us down 9-0 in the third quarter, when Unitas refused to kick on a fourth and one at the Lions' 47. Alan "the Horse" Ameche became literally a "Flying Hoss," leaping over his blocker and a Lion or two to reach the 44. We galloped on for three touchdowns and the game ended 21-9. We had five interceptions, one of which was mine.

Being the title holders, we figured everyone would be gunning for us. But we didn't expect the Bears to bring in such heavy artillery. They bombed us with 26 points during the first three quarters, before we began our usual last-minute attack. The only problem was that time ran out after we got 21 points. George Halas walked off the field grinning like a cat that has just caught the most-wanted mouse. If we could have just had a 30-minute warm-up scrimmage with the Bears before the game!

When would we ever learn?

Naturally in the return match with the Lions in Detroit, we were behind 24-14 in the third quarter, when Andy Nelson intercepted and ran the ball back for a score. A Lion muttered, "Some guys get their Christmas real early." The Lions were still ahead 24-21 midway in the fourth period when Unitas connected with Berry on a third and ten at the Colt 47. Raymond took it at the Lion 40, ran crossfield, faked out two Lions, got good blocking from Richardson and Mutscheller, and went in for the go-ahead score.

But sadness dampened our joy in the locker room. Coach Ewbank told us that NFL Commissioner Bert Bell was critically ill. Weeb asked me to include him in the locker room prayer.

We could hardly wait to get back to the Bears who had earlier defeated us. But after managing only one touchdown in the first half, some of the guys figured there was a monkey in the woodpile. Unitas and the offense had never been so frustrated with only one touchdown out of six scoring opportunities in the first half. I'm not saying the Bears knew our signals, but I'm not saying they didn't. Unitas said, "They have a better book on us than we have ourselves."

John was using a color signal system. When he came up to take the snap from center, he looked over the defense and called a color. The offense knew certain colors were live: yellow, for example. If John called "yellow, 34, 4-3, ready set," this meant he had changed the play. A run might become a pass or vice versa. What looked fishy was that the Bears moved into different defensive formations when Unitas gave the color.

You can bet our offense changed their check-off colors during the half. Weeb told us to keep telling ourselves we were trailing by two scores rather than ahead by one. He got his point across. After Lenny Moore got the second of two touchdowns, I intercepted a pass (my second of the game) and ran the ball back to the Bear 14. The offense took it from there and the game ended 21-7.

On the plane back, Coach Ewbank worked on a new signal system. Dimitri Spassoff, the Colt's new assistant Bulgarian trainer, had his own idea. He offered to teach Unitas the check-offs in Bulgarian.

Now with a three-and-one record we were tied with the Packers and the 49'ers for the Western Conference lead. And the Packers were next.

We sent them back to Wisconsin glum to the tune of 38-21. Ameche and Berry each crossed the goal line twice and my line-backing buddy Bill Pellington ran an interception back for the fifth touchdown.

This victory left us in the company of only the 49'ers at the top of the Western Conference.

A week later and the 49'ers had the peak all to themselves. The Cleveland Browns punctured our pride 38-31.

Unitas threw for 397 yards against Cleveland but Jimmy Brown was still too much. He ran 32 of Cleveland's 42 rushing plays for 178 yards and 5 touchdowns. We tried every defense we had from a three-man to an eight-man line. But the man from Syracuse kept wriggling, dancing, and squirming his way through. Again and again he got Cleveland off the hook.

Our "Big Daddy" Lipscomb made tackles all over the field, and picked up the men afterward according to his custom. But once, he knocked down Jimmy Brown and failed to pick him up. Jimmy asked, "What's the matter 'Big Daddy'? Are you mad at me?" "No," Big Daddy said, "I just forgot, and I am tired."

So we were in second place. But we didn't feel worried because the "weak" Redskins were next.

Yipes!

They ambushed us. We didn't score for 41 minutes and 50 seconds and then three touchdowns and a field goal were not enough. The 'Skins won it on a last second 46-yard field goal set up by an interception. They hadn't scored that many points in all of their six previous games! Don't ask how many!

I was sick, sick, sick after the game — not physically, but mentally. Losing to the Browns a week before had been no disgrace. But losing to the 'Skins was. I had moved too slow, missed tackles, and in general, played a sloppy game. I did something I had never done before. I turned my weekly pay check back to the club. The front office must have agreed that I had done lousy for they kept it a few days before giving it back to me.

Now we were two games behind the 49'ers whom we were scheduled to play twice before the season ended.

And I wanted so much to help the Colts win the championship for Junior. The doctor had said the baby would arrive in early March. We felt this to be a blessing from the Lord.

I always feel sorry for the guys who must play a team rebounding from a heartbreaking loss. This time it was the Packers who had to play us the "week after." Ordinarily, the Packers might have beaten us. Bart Starr and his teammates gained 416 total yards. Jim Taylor ran for three touchdowns. But after losing to the 'Skins, we were not to be denied this one. Our offense accounted for 516 yards. Unitas was not intercepted a single time. Starr had three passes stolen. I grabbed one and paired with Gino Marchetti to knock Starr off balance and set up another. Still the Packers' Coach Lombardi said, "We've played worse and won."

San Francisco lost to the Bears, putting us only one game behind them. And delight of delights, the 49'ers were due to call on us the next Sunday. A win could put us back on top. A loss was not to be considered.

I'm not much to talk about key plays in any game (I think every play is important), but I suppose you could say the key play of this game was the opening kick-off. From then until the final gun sounded we did everything but bury the hapless 49'ers. Our offense piled up almost three times as much yardage as Y. A. Tittle and his boys accumulated. We mixed up the defensive patterns quite a bit to keep Tittle guessing. Five or six times, Big Daddy Lipscomb played back from his line position while we linebackers blitzed. In effect he acted like a linebacker and laid back for the trap and draw plays and the screen passes. Speaking of passes, Dick Szymanski stole Tittle's first pass and his next-to-last throw in the game. The score: 49-14.

This put us back in a first place tie with the team we had just defeated. We knew that every one of the three games left, two with the Rams and one with the 49'ers, was crucial.

A long time before, Horace Greeley had advised young men

to go west and seek their fortunes. The Colts had gone west and lost 20 out of 22 tries. Before we went west we had a home game with the Rams.

We slammed the Rams 35-21 in the first game, even though Ram quarterback Billy Wade threw for more yardage than Unitas.

The 49'ers recouped to beat Cleveland 21-20 and continued off to the west coast and two final games.

The next game against the 49'ers was our biggest of the season. We had to beat the 49'ers who we knew would be out to pay us back for the Baltimore drubbing. We had to break a jinx of 11 straight Colt losses in Kezar Stadium.

We did it with John Unitas breaking Sid Luckman's old 1943 record of most scoring passes in a season. I pulled down two of six Colt pass interceptions — the first one off the arm of my old nemesis, John Brodie. I ran it back 26 yards to the 'Frisco 32 and from there the offense took it in. My second swipe came off gutty Y. A. Tittle who came into the game still afflicted by injuries suffered in our previous contest at Baltimore. I grabbed this one as Tittle was smelling pay dirt. Unitas took over and threw a 64-yard payoff pass that put him ahead of Sid Luckman.

Now if we could beat the Rams in the final game, we would be Western Conference champs again and eligible to play for the NFL title. The Giants had again clinched the Eastern Conference.

The game turned out to be a heart-stopper.

After seven straight game losses, the Rams came back and battled us to a 26-24 lead in the fourth quarter. Twelve of our points had come off Steve Myhra's golden toe. Once I goofed by running on the field without my helmet on and lost the Colts a time-out. Then the Rams got a showing of that old Colt last quarter magic.

Within five minutes the following happened: Unitas threw a nine-yard scoring pass to Jerry Richardson. Dick Szymanski picked off an interception and galloped fifteen yards for a score while I sat on the ground and clapped my hands and yelled, "Go, Dick, go." Carl Taseff picked up the ball on the Colt one after the Rams missed a field goal and made a 99-yard runback for another score. Final tally: 45-26.

I want to tell you that I made my seventh interception, giving me a tie with teammate Miit Davis and Pittsburgh's Dean Derby for most interceptions in the NFL that year. So far as I know this is the only time a linebacker has ever tied for the league lead.

The season's tally showed the Colts had rewritten the club record book on scoring, passes thrown, passes caught, and touchdown passes caught. Club interceptions amounted to forty, just two shy of the all-time NFL record. Seventeen of these were by Bill, Dick and myself. This must be a league record for linebackers.

But we didn't stop to meditate on such figures before the Giant game. We knew that Conerly and his cronies would be out to avenge their 1958 sudden-death disaster. Besides Conerly, the Giants had almost their entire squad back, which included Gifford, Rote, Schnelker, and Huff, the NFL's "Lineman of the Year." Vince Lombardi, the former Giant assistant who had gone to Green Bay, rated the game a toss-up and said he was anticipating a championship in Packer land the next year.

A few people worried about the Giants new reserve quarterback, George Shaw, whom they had bought from the Colts earlier in the year. They worried because Shaw had vital information on our offensive strategy.

The title affair turned out to be a typical Colt game. Except for one brilliant play, the offense didn't do much for three quarters. Then Unitas spun to his left, faked, then swiveled right and saw that no one was open. He swiveled another time or two until he saw Lenny Moore had picked up a little daylight from his double coverage. John, whom a sports writer called "the greatest hoodwinker since Houdini," threw a perfect pass right into the breadbasket and Lenny took it in for the score. However, the Giants' Pat Summerall kicked three field goals and the fourth quarter began with the New Yorkers leading 9-7.

No one gives up on the Colts in the fourth quarter; certainly not in Baltimore; certainly not on a score this close, even with the Giants moving in for a kill. Our defense squeezed the Giants into a fourth and inches situation on our 28. We told one another in the huddle, "Let's get the ball and the offense will score." The Giants didn't go for the field goal. Conerly gave it to Webster, but smart Alex hit a stone wall and our offense took over.

With the fans screaming, "Take us in, John," Unitas did just that, making six points on his own muscle. The conversion gave us a five-point lead.

Who said interceptions don't count? Handy Andy Nelson pilfered Brother Conerly's pass and set up the offense for another score. The Colts rolled on to a 31-16 triumph.

We headed for the dressing room whooping and hollering, like the winners we were. When the door was closed, I led the guys in the Lord's prayer. Weeb Ewbank said, "I want to thank all of you. You're great. And we're going on and on."

Vice-President Nixon came in to offer his congratulations. Then the writers poured in to get their quotes.

It was another great day. Winning two titles in a row seemed just dandy to me since the doctor had just told us Marsha would have twins.

Nope, I didn't make the League's official "All-Pro" team, although six of my teammates did — Unitas (again the NFL's "Player of the Year"), Berry, Parker, Spinney, Marchetti, and Lipscomb. The UPI named me to the "All-Pro" second team defense. In my darker moments, I wondered if I could make "All-Pro" with 70 interceptions.

11

"A Very Hard Year"

I've never enjoyed waiting for anything. January, after the 1959 title game, seemed 365 days long. I spoke all over the country, and near Baltimore, hoping I would be around when the babies were born.

Marsha's mother came to help out. There are a lot of jokes about mothers-in-law, but I had no cracks when she arrived. She was plenty welcome.

Early Tuesday morning, February 9, Marsha went in a taxi to the hospital, because I was in Canada on a speaking engagement. I really was disappointed because I wasn't with her, but I learned a lesson. I had been speaking 5 or 6 times a week and not sharing enough of my life with my wife.

When I called from Canada the doctor told me, "Mr. Shinnick, you are the father of identical twin boys."

Although I knew twins were coming, it was still a bomb. I vowed to become a good family man.

We named them Peter and Joel. Peter, after the impetuous Apostle Peter. Joel, after the Old Testament prophet. Marsha has always said that I am like the apostle in temperament.

I came home the next day and they let me see the boys. I grinned and said something like, "I hope they both play on the same defense. That would really confuse an opponent."

Two or three days after their birth, I got the first word that Peter had a problem. The pediatrician thought there was an obstruction in the intestines and said they would like to do exploratory surgery.

Marsha came home from the hospital the day of the operation. I was with her since there was nothing I could do at the hospital. The phone rang while she was taking a shower. "Mr. Shinnick, we are terribly, terribly sorry," the doctor said. "Your little Peter didn't make it."

I told Marsha. It was the hardest thing I ever did.

Later we learned that the baby had picked up a staph infection in the hospital which developed into a fatal perforated ulcer.

Through the years I've had people ask me how I reconcile tragedy and the love of God. My answer has always been Romans 8:28, "We know that all things work together for good to them that love God. . . ." This tells me that there is no catastrophe on God's level of thinking, only on ours. God knows so much more than we do.

I don't mean to imply that the death of little Peter was easy for us to accept. We tried to give little Joel a double helping of love and were thankful for the healthy baby we could bring home. And we prayed and read Scripture together as always.

Our faith had never meant so much.

I continued to do a lot of speaking that spring. More calls came in than I could fill.

Occasionally someone would suggest a hot business opportunity and say, "Shinnick, you can make more money by giving your time to this." My answer was, "I'm sure I could, but my time belongs to God, and He is giving me these opportunities to speak." As during past off-seasons, I always told my audiences that I came to them as a Christian layman to speak of my faith.

Raymond Berry was one who never doubted the worth of what I was doing. We had become close friends and had begun rooming together on road trips during 1959. We got along fine even though I preferred to watch TV at night while he liked to study. Good old accommodating Raymond would simply stuff in ear plugs and dive into his play book.

We talked about the values we shared. Both of us shared similar moral convictions. Raymond did curse occasionally, which I didn't. My strongest oath was, "What the rip!" and "You're a quack." His father was a high school football coach and a Sunday school teacher.

In early July, 1960, I met Ray at National Guard camp.

One evening we were talking about religious beliefs and he

said, "Don, it seems to me that you believe in Jesus Christ as strongly as I believe in God. What's the difference?"

I tried to explain the difference as I saw it. "We know there is a God who created and sustains the cosmos — a God who is eternal and over all. But just knowing God by intellect doesn't satisfy our souls. The Bible tells us in I John that we can only know God in a personal soul-satisfying way through trusting and believing in His Son, Jesus Christ. Then I turned to him and said, "Raymond, if I were to judge, I would wonder if you have accepted Christ as your Saviour."

"But I was baptized and received into the church at ten," he countered.

About a week later we talked about Christ again when we were outside Alan Ameche's Hamburger Place. This time I asked him, "Raymond, would you like to become the Christian that the Bible talks about by believing in Christ?"

He said, "Yes," and we bowed our heads and I said a prayer that he repeated — something like this, "Dear God, please forgive my sins. I now believe in and receive Jesus Christ as my Saviour."

I read to him John 1:12, "But as many as received him, to them gave he power to become the sons of God, even to them that believe on his name." Then I assured him that if he had really believed in Jesus, the Holy Spirit would live in him, help him understand the Bible, and give him strength to glorify Christ. I also read to him I John 1:9, the Scripture that promises to Christians forgiveness for daily sins as they confess them. Then we thanked God that He did this.

What happened to Raymond? Here's his report: "The changes that took place after that were gradual, day by day, a little at a time. For the first time I began to realize what a sinner I was. Prayer became an everyday experience. Studying the Word of God became a real joy, and verses that before had no meaning suddenly did. As I looked back to where I stood in the sight of God before that July night when I prayed, there gradually came the awareness that I had been a lost soul. Before then Christ had not meant any more to me than any other person in history. There had been no connection in my mind between Jesus Christ and salvation or even what salvation meant. And I don't ever remember wondering just why Christ came into the world, and what is the significance of His life, death, and resurrection. I can only say now that I am so thankful to Him for saving my soul from the eternal fire and letting me know that He loves me."

Right after he finished his National Guard duty, Raymond got another pass thrower on August 20 — I mean a wife. He married sweet Sally Ann Crook, a Texas gal he had met while coaching at Baylor during the past spring. I accused him of marrying her just to have someone to throw him passes when no one else would. Of course he denied that. But it seemed that every time I went to their house, they were out in the back yard with the football. Seriously, Raymond and Sally make an ideal couple, and her pass throwing shows how serious Raymond is about football.

I've often thought that when the Lord was handing out the talent, He gave more football ability to some guys than Raymond, but He never gave anyone more determination than this champion. What he may lack in blinding straightaway speed, he makes up for in quickness and an uncanny ability to be where the ball is thrown. If you've ever seen him bite the dust for a low pass, leap to snatch a brown blur out of the air, or make a corkscrew twist to grab the ball before stepping out of bonds, you know that he's a champion. Even if he doesn't look like some people's idea of a football player off the field, he is really a mild mannered "Clark Kent."

During training camp I think the guys began to sense that something had happened to Raymond. It wasn't so much a change of habits, for Raymond had always had a good moral reputation among the Colts. It was what he would say at an appropriate moment. Like at the dinner table he might say, "Joe, have you ever thought about Who gave you that body and the ability to play football?"

We won three and lost three in the 1960 pre-season games. The Packers under Lombardi had a perfect 6-0 record. But Lombardi picked us to be champs again in the Western Conference with the Bears coming in second. "Our Packers don't have enough depth," he said, "but should we get by without crippling injuries, we could be trouble for anybody."

No team in NFL history had then won three titles in a row. A good many people, besides Lombardi, thought we might be that team. However, Bill Wallace of the *New York Herald Tribune* said that should our dynasty collapse, Green Bay would be the new leader in the Western half of the NFL.

We still had substantially the same team as a year before. L. G. "Long Gone" Dupre had gone to the newest club in the NFL, the Dallas Cowboys, who were starting with Tom Landry as head coach and plucky Eddie LeBaron as the starting quarterback. Don Meredith from SMU was just then beginning his rookie year at Dallas.

And the upstart AFL had organized and bid for a piece of the pro football pie with eight teams.

We opened against the Redskins and throttled them 20-0. Our defense set a new club record by allowing the 'Skins only 113 yards. The 'Skins rookie quarterback Eagle Day just didn't have the stuff of the little gentleman Eddie LeBaron who had been traded to the Cowboys.

Gino Marchetti and Art Donovan, the two "old men" of the Colts — 33 and 35 respectively — bulldozed the Washington blockers. They were smarting from a press remark about their age. I swiped one pass.

We next walloped the Bears 42-7 on seven interceptions off Zeke Bratkowski. Rookie Bob Boyd from the University of Oklahoma, Andy Nelson, and I got two each. I laughed as I ran out of bounds with one interception because no one could hit me there. Both Berry and Unitas finished the game ahead of their 1959 league-leading pace. After the game, the press learned that Unitas had played with a cracked vertebra suffered in an exhibition game.

This win put us all alone at the top of the Western Conference. We could smell that three-titles-in-a-row record.

Whoa and woe! The Packers took us to the slaughter house 35-21 with Bart Starr passing, Paul Hornung and Jim Taylor running, and Vince Lombardi grinning from the sidelines. Hadn't Lombardi picked us to win the Conference? Now with a two and-one record we were tied with Green Bay and two other teams.

Giddap, Colts! We came back the next week and knocked off the Rams. Lenny "Sputnik" Moore exploded (and that's the word for his running) for four touchdowns. Just to show that Raymond Berry is human, I'll report that he missed a pass without a Ram defender near enough to deflect or hinder him. He said afterward, "We didn't have our timing right."

"Hold it," the Lions said as they reined us in at Detroit, despite 11 catches by Raymond Berry for 186 yards, including a touchdown pass caught while falling over backward in the end zone. But the Lions were lucky or we made mistakes, depending on how you want to classify a fumble and an interception. Preacher Bill Glass from Baylor recovered the fumble on our ten at a critical time in the fourth quarter when we might have gone ahead. And Dick "Night Train" Lane, who covered Lenny Moore like a second skin, intercepted a floating pass from Unitas and ran 80 yards back for a touchdown. Jim Martin's three long-range field goals, one for 52 yards, were a big plus in the Lions' 30-17 win. I blocked Martin's try for a fourth three-pointer.

The loss dropped us to third place, behind Green Bay and Chicago. But we still had hopes. Beating easy-mark Dallas, the rookie team and our next opponent, would give us a four-and-two record, the mark we had held at the same time in 1959.

The game was a 45-7 romp with Raymond Berry scooping in three touchdown passes in the Cotton Bowl stadium where he had played during his SMU days. I made two interceptions, giving me five steals for the season, and a tie for the league leadership in interceptions with Andy Nelson.

Wow!

We beat the Packers next in a hair-raising finish. After leading 21-0, the Pack mushed back to tie it at 24-24 in the fourth quarter. With a fourth-down-inches-to-go situation on the Green Bay 38, Unitas faked a handoff to fullback Ameche, whirled and threw a wide, flat pass to Lenny Moore. First down on the Packers 15. Then Berry took a pass on the 10-yard line, did a ballet along the sidelines, staying inbounds by inches, dodged two Packer tackles, and went in for the go-ahead score, Raymond's third scoring reception for the day. Someone suggested after the game, which ended 38-24, that the end zone be named "the Berry patch."

That win put us back in first place in the Western Conference, a half game ahead of Green Bay.

Take us to Chicago.

We figured the Bears would still be nursing their wounded pride from the 42-7 licking they had received earlier in Baltimore. They were — and how! I think some of them remembered me laughing after I had intercepted a pass in the previous game.

They led us 20-17 with a minute and 37 seconds to go. Unitas heaved the football just as 500 pounds of Doug Atkins and Bill George hit him like a couple of wild grizzlies. The pass was complete for a first down on the Bear 35.

John lay still. The Colt trainers rushed to his aid. His mouth was ripped and the bridge of his nose torn apart. "I'll make it . . . I'll make it," he kept mumbling as they bandaged his wounds.

He got up and continued to play. The next two plays netted seven yards. On third down Bill George hit him for an 11-yard loss to the Bears 39. Fourth and fourteen with 27 seconds to go.

The blood was caking on his puffed and swollen face as he lined up behind center Buzz Nutter. Everyone in the stadium knew he had two options: call for a field goal or try a desperate pass. I doubt if anyone expected John to go for three points which would only bring a tie. It wasn't in keeping with his character.

He barked a play known as "66-take off." This called for Lenny Moore to feint in at an angle, then beat the half-back, J. C. Caroline, if he could.

Baltimore Sun writer Jim Ellis had said Lenny was fast enough to run between raindrops without getting wet. He would have done it that day if it had been raining. He got ahead of Caroline at the goal line and caught Unitas' pass in the end zone. The conversion made the score 24-20.

Unitas said afterward, "It was the toughest game I ever played."

Jim Parker spoke for us all when he said, "I'd rather be cut and bleeding myself than see John hurt. He's the greatest yet."

My dad and stepmother, who live in Chicago, came around to congratulate me. "John Unitas is the one," I told them proudly.

We stayed in first place, a half game ahead of Green Bay who beat Dallas the same day.

Then the bottom fell out! How did it happen? That's what we are still asking ourselves. How does a team win the way we had just won over the Bears and then lose the next four games? Some say the physical beating that we took in the Chicago game had something to do with it.

The 49'ers whacked us 30-22 over five interceptions and three fumbles. "You don't make mistakes like that and get away with it in the NFL," Weeb Ewbank said. The loss must have embarrassed Colts' owner Carrol Rosenbloom who had Bobby Kennedy, the brother of the man just elected President, as his special guest.

Even with this setback, we were still the front runners in the Western Conference, a half game ahead of the Bears and a game ahead of the Packers.

The Lions were next. What a heartbreaker.

With 22 seconds to go in the game, and a third-and-one situation, we were behind 13-8. Unitas lined a low pass toward the corner of the end zone. "Night Train" Lane was running with Lenny Moore, when suddenly Lenny ignited an extra engine and leaped out in front to make a diving full-length catch on the ends of his fingers. The conversion made it 15-13.

The fans poured out on the field and surrounded Lenny. A fight erupted between both teams on the field. Some of the fans were probably in it, too. I think I got under the bench.

The officials got the fans off the field, but not back in their seats. The Colts kicked off and the Lions ran the ball back to their 35.

Seven seconds to go.

We threw up a defense that we had not worked on in practice, something we learned not to do again. We had a four-man rush, with the defensive backs spread out deep to stop a bomb.

Morrall's receiver, Jim Gibbons, got through our defensive backfield and went all the way for the winning touchdown. In seven seconds sudden life had turned into sudden death for us.

I mumbled something like, "Amen, Brother Ben," and began walking across the field. I ran into the Lions' Bill Glass, now with the Baltimore Colts, and said, "Praise God."

Bill said, "What do you mean? How can you praise God after that?"

"Because," I said, "we're Christians and know there's more to life than winning or losing a football game."

On Monday I clipped Psalm 145:18, the verse for the day in the *Baltimore News-Post*: "The Lord is nigh unto all them that call upon him, to all that call upon him in truth."

Would you believe that with a 6-4 record we were still in first place, though tied with the Packers and the 49'ers? The Bears were half a game behind and the Lions only a game back.

We had two games on the West Coast left to play. But we had to win without Alan Ameche, who was out for the season with a leg injury from the Lion game.

It happened to be my turn to write the weekly player's column in the *Baltimore News-Post*. I wrote, "When I lose confidence in our team, I'll quit. We can do it. We believe in each other. Anything worth anything in life never comes easy."

We battled the Rams with Raymond Berry playing with a pulled muscle and Art Donovan limping with one leg swollen to twice its normal size. I still have bad memories of Billy Wade running down the sidelines on a rollout and four of us trying to chase him. We got caught on a blitz. His touchdown made the difference and the Rams won 10-3. It was the first time in many a moon that Unitas had not thrown a scoring pass. When John heard that he had broken Sammy Baugh's total yardage mark for a single season, he said, "Take it back. We lost."

The 49'ers beat us, too. We ended up six and six in fourth place. The Packers took the Western Conference, but were defeated by the Eastern champion Philadelphia Eagles in the title game.

Naturally, I didn't go to the Pro Bowl.

No doubt about it. It was a hard year. I lost a son at the beginning and the Colts lost a title at the end. The two bright spots were the good health of little Joel and the conversion of Raymond Berry.

One little incident stood out at the close of the season. A husky telephone lineman told Raymond at a church banquet, "What you said in a newspaper article helped a friend of mine become a Christian."

Raymond told me and I remembered. We had been flying home from a game when a sportswriter had asked Raymond for a statement of his faith. Being a new Christian, Raymond came to me for suggestions. I suggested that he simply tell what had happened to him spiritually.

We knew that the past season hadn't been a total loss and we prayed that our witness would count for even more in 1961.

Win or lose.

12

"Lombardi's Legions"

Early in 1961 Marsha and I and the baby left for California where I was to attend Fuller Theological Seminary in Pasadena, California. Before leaving, I told the press, "I am convinced that learning to know more about the Bible and about God is something that can benefit more than just ministers. It will help me if I coach, or with anything else I may do."

While attending seminary, I spoke to church and football groups two or three times each week and taught a co-ed young people's Sunday school class at the First Baptist Church of Burbank. I led them in a systematic study of four channels through which God reveals Himself to the world: (1) His Son, Jesus Christ; (2) His Holy Spirit; (3) His inspired Word, the Bible; (4) His people.

Tempus fugus. That was a happy four months. I finished the semester's studies and, on the way back from California to my training camp, we stopped in Detroit where I participated in the first Fellowship of Christian Athletes' rally in that city. A bunch of great guys were there: Gail Cogdill, Jim Ninowski, and Bill Glass of the Detroit Lions; Bill Wade, the new Chicago Bear quarterback; Bobby Richardson, and Raymond Berry. The rally took place at a large metropolitan church.

Both Raymond and I had heard about FCA, but until this time had not spoken too much for them. I had known about it from its beginning in 1955 — I was even in the first movie they made. We were eager to help them out whenever we could.

The idea for FCA had sprung from a church talk made in 1947 in Stillwater, Oklahoma by a young coach named Don McClanen. He spoke on "Making My Vocation Christian."

McClanen, from Eastern Oklahoma A&M, said later, "The talk caused me to stop and think on how in the coaching business I could make the most effective Christian witness."

Eight years later FCA was chartered by several Christian leaders, mostly ex-athletes who saw it as a channel for a Christian witness in the athletic world. Among these first supporters were Dr. Louis H. Evans, Sr., Dr. Elton Trueblood, Dr. Sam Shoemaker, Branch Rickey, Donn Moomaw, "Deacon" Dan Towler, Gary Demarest, and Roe Johnston. By 1962, FCA had a headquarters office in Kansas City, an expanding summer conference ministry, and a traveling squad of Christian athletes who were willing to give their time in speaking and witnessing for Christ. Raymond and I both felt that FCA held enormous potential for Christian witness in and beyond the athletic world.

A good looking bunch of rookies showed up for the '61 training camp. Two of the most promising were Tom Matte from Ohio State, whom we nicknamed "Squeaky" because his voice became shrill when he tried to talk loud, and Jerry Hill from the University of Wyoming. Two other good men that I remember from that camp came from the Pittsburgh Steelers: Billy Ray Smith and Jimmy Orr, whom the Colts hoped would add more depth in the pass rush and pass-receiving department. And the 13-year veteran Joe Perry came from the 49'ers who had sent Y. A. Tittle, another old-timer, to the Giants.

There were a few losses from the 1960 Colts squad, but except for Alan Ameche, retired by an injury, and the trading of Big Daddy to Pittsburgh, we were intact. This was a tough trade to understand, but that's part of the game.

There was the usual crowd of people, mostly little boys, hanging around for autographs and a peek at their favorite players. I told some of the players, "If you want to get rid of them, just have Weeb Ewbank send me home. They're all here for my autograph." Well, one of them did come for that purpose.

I usually add a Scripture verse to my name when signing autographs. One day I signed Don Shinnick, John 3:16, for a towhead. When the kid kept hanging around, I asked him who else did he expect to see? He said, "Johnny Unitas. You wrote right here John 3:16. That's when he's supposed to arrive, isn't it — 3:16 p.m.?"

Our title hopes were up again. We figured we had been as good as Green Bay, Detroit, and the other clubs who finished ahead of us the past season with our misfortune coming from injuries and bad breaks.

Raymond Berry was still recuperating from a knee operation when we took on the Rams in the season opener. Our passing game showed his absence. Old pro Joe Perry, whom the 49'ers had thought was over the hill, saved the day by rushing for 106 yards in 18 carries. The Colt defensive star was another old pro, Gino Marchetti, who led our line and came up with the Ram fumble that set up our offense to tie the score. We went on to win 27-24 after knocking the Rams' QB Zeke Bratkowski flat in the fourth quarter.

I could have had a fight in the fourth quarter after breaking up a pass to a Ram rookie. The freshman punched at me after the ball fell away. I turned away. A writer said that I "turned the other cheek." I don't know about that, but I do know my philosophy is that it's better to be a live chicken than a dead hero — at least on the football field.

The Lions took us by a point, 16-15, the next week. With Berry still out, our passing game stayed below par. Pellington and Taseff sat the second half out with injuries and the Lions won with a field goal in the last four minutes. Billy Ray Smith and I each recovered a fumble.

Our turn came the next week when we beat the rookie Vikings with a 52-yard field goal on the last play of the game. The Vikes really had their horns out for us. But Lenny Moore buttoned up three Unitas passes for touchdowns, one a 72-yard bomb, and Raymond Berry was back and grabbed six passes. Yeah, and I recovered a loose ball following a blocked punt.

We didn't get to see the little sharp-eyed rookie from Georgia perform for the Vikes. Fancy Fran the Scrambling Man (Fran Tarkenton) sat on the bench and watched Old Colt George Shaw run the show for the Minnesota offense.

I'd just as soon forget the next game. The Packers did everything but pack us in tin cans and send us home as horse meat.

I think we made about 75 per cent of our total number of mistakes for the season in that game. We missed tackles, blocks, ran bad patterns, fumbled three times, had six interceptions, fouled up defensive coverages, and well, you name it, we did it. Not to discredit Starr, Hornung, and Taylor, but I think any team could have beaten us. The score: 45-7.

When it rains it pours.

The Bears beat us 24-10 to drop us into fifth place in the Western Conference. The score was tied 10-10 until Willie Gallimore ran a screen pass 84 yards to a touchdown. But one bit of Colt gallantry didn't go unnoticed in the press. Raymond and the Bear's Dave Whitsell both went sprawling on a pass play. After Raymond was up and walking away, he turned and saw Whitsell still on the ground. He ran back. leaned down, and asked, "You all right, Davey?" After the game Whitsell said, "Raymond is the best — a fine gentleman."

A field goal by Steve Myhra, the farmer from North Dakota, in the last eight seconds gave us a 17-14 win over Detroit. A Baltimore writer said that after the game, I prayed, "Lord, bless that farmer with the big leg." As I remember, I did.

Glub! Glub! Glub! The Bears put us under water by a point, that difference coming from a blocked point-after try. The high pass from center probably allowed the Halas heroes an extra second or two which was all they needed. A lot of people claimed that poor officiating deprived us of three more touchdowns. I'm not condemning the gallant men in stripes, but with all the holding of our pass receivers, I thought sometimes the Bears wanted a wrestling match.

The defeat put us below .500 for the first time since I had joined the Colts.

Glory be! We rose from the grave and beat the Packers 45-21. Everything went right. Lenny Moore! Man, was he something! Once he jerked his foot loose from Hank Gremminger, bounced off five more Packers, and exploded down the sidelines for a 38-yard touchdown. A great run!

What happened?

That's what we were asking ourselves after the cellar-dwelling Vikings upset us 28-20. Perhaps the question should have been,

"Where'd he go?" Francy Fran the Scrambling Man, that is. This time he didn't sit on the bench. Now, where was he? We saw him and we didn't see him. We saw only gloom in the dressing room.

The clouds lifted. We took the Cardinals 16-0 and the Redskins 27-6. Lenny Moore looked so good in the Redskins game (122 yards for 6 rushes), that he caught the praise of George Preston Marshall, the Redskins' owner. Mr. Marshall had the dubious reputation of having never hired a Negro player.

Of the three games left, we won two and lost one. We played for little but pride against the 49'ers in the last game, but I'll always remember it.

We were only three points ahead and it appeared John Brodie was going to get the go-ahead touchdown in the closing minutes when I intercepted on the 14. The Colts' offense then ran out the clock.

We ended up with eight wins and six losses, tied for third place in the Western Conference. Weeb Ewbank was feeling the heat from some Colt fans who couldn't understand why the Colts had gone two years without a title. But in 1961 it was all Green Bay. The Packers took the Western Conference 11-3 and walloped the Giants 37-0 for the NFL title.

But the debunkers were saying that neither the Packers nor any NFL team could be declared world champions until they played and beat the winners of the American Football League.

This year wasn't much different for me than 1961. I studied at Fuller Seminary during the spring, did a lot of speaking, made appearances for charity groups, and tried to keep the spirits of the guys up when we were losing. "Here comes Shinnick," they would say, "coming in on a joke or a prayer." One writer described me as irreverent toward everything except religion. I would hardly say that, but I've always felt that when you can't smile, you're ready for the undertaker. Leslie Flynn wrote in *Serve Him With Mirth*: "Why is it that of all the creatures in the world only man can laugh? Why, on hearing something funny, does a person throw back his head, open his mouth, and with chest heaving to and fro as though in convulsions, laugh as his breath pumps out in explosive puffs? The answer is because God has made him so."

We all felt part of the fun had left the club when Art Donovan retired. We knew he would be hard to replace as a fall-guy among the practical jokers. Some of the guys even sent him off with a bang. They tied a small explosive to a tire of his car and it exploded when he left camp.

I got a muscle pull in camp and for awhile wore a red shirt, the badge of the untouchable. I figured some of the guys might be color blind so I stuck a strip of tape across my shoulders with the plea printed in large letters, "Don't hit me — I'm sick."

After beating the Rams' 30-27 in our opener, we went to Minneapolis. On Saturday night Berry, Tarkenton, and I teamed up to give a witness to a Youth For Christ rally of 2,000 teen-agers. Fran really wowed them with his testimony. "Becoming a Christian was the greatest thrill I ever had, greater than any touchdown pass."

On the football field the next day it was a different story. Fran spent a good deal of time on the field — we (mostly Gino Marchetti and Billy Ray Smith) dumped him nine times for 86 yards of losses! For the first time in nine games he failed to throw a single touchdown pass. Fran seemed deliberately to avoid throwing passes in my neighborhood. Even without our two Lennys — (Lyles and Moore, both out with injuries), the Colts romped to a 34-7 win. I guess it all goes to prove that Christians can be closer than brothers except when they're playing football on opposite teams.

The next game with the Lions was one of *those* days — or perhaps I should say *daze*. Milt Plum went for a foot on a quarterback sneak to get the first down and got 45 yards and a score. Once we played "drop the handkerchief" with pass interceptions. First, Dick LeBeau picked off a Unitas aerial. Two plays later I grabbed a pass off Milt Plum (I had a second interception at another point in the game). On the next play Alex Karras grabbed Unitas' pass after John's arm was hit. Then the Lions stopped the circus and went in for a touchdown. And once Unitas fell down on slippery turf right in front of the goal line. Detroit won it on breaks 29-20, holding us to a two-and-one record for the year.

We lost three of our next four games, dropping contests to the 49'ers, the Bears and the Packers, and winning over the Cleveland Browns.

Jim Brown didn't have one of his best days. He fumbled once, which for him was about as rare as a warm day in Green Bay during December. He was involved once in a confuse-the-oppostion scoring play. Ninowski, the Browns quarterback, handed off to him. Jim lateraled back to Ninowski. Just as a Colt tackler moved in, Ninowski passed to Dick Kreitling on the Colt five and Kreitling stepped across for the score—the familiar flea-flicker play. Despite such antics as these, we won 36-14.

We lost to the Packers on the Sunday after the Cuban missile crisis. At midseason this left Lombardi's men undefeated and looking as if they'd go all the way again.

We split four games in November, winning from the 49'ers and Rams, and losing to the Packers and Bears. The Baltimore fans began booing Weeb Ewbank. None of us wanted to be in his shoes. Baltimore is a win town. The fans will excuse a coach for one losing season, they will tolerate him for two, but they're ready to help him pack his bags if he loses three years in a row.

The 49'ers used three quarterbacks in the first game which we won 22-3. Our defense did it this time with Bob Boyd coming in for two interceptions. Raymond Berry was in for only two plays. When he came back to the room for prayer and Bible study with me, he said, "Man, it's hard to thank the Lord for being in on only two plays." I knew Raymond had been having a struggle to keep from feeling badly toward Weeb Ewbank for benching him the past four or five games.

We stayed on the Coast for the next Sunday's game with the Rams.

The Rams game was something of a repeat of the 49'ers game, except they got a safety instead of a field goal. Raymond Berry had a few good receptions. Unitas looked much better than he had the week before. I grabbed off a long Zeke Bratkowski pass intended for Carroll Dale which set the Colts up for a touchdown. Carroll, now with the Packers, is a leader in the Fellowship of Christian Athletes.

We came back from the West Coast feeling good. For the first time in our memories an East Coast team had travelled to the West Coast for two games and kept the opposition from crossing the goal line.

Our third game in November was sad — awfully sad. We lost by four — 17-13 — to Green Bay with Herb Adderly making a 103-yard kickoff return. Our depression even seemed to affect the four-engine charter plane as we came in for a landing. One engine began to sputter and backfire.

Our fourth game was sadder still. The Bears beat us 57-0. I'll spare you the trauma of reading the details.

We were like a satellite spinning out of control during that game. I felt like joining the mob that was booing us. Man, were we lousy. Well, at least we helped Bill Wade lead the NFL in pass completions that year. "Bill, did you ever thank us for that?"

December was a little better. We lost the first game (14-21, to the Lions) and won the last two.

"Lenny Moore Day" was celebrated during our next home game. He and his family were showered with special gifts that showed the appreciation of the Baltimore fans. He deserved it.

You should see the stack of clippings I've saved from that game which we won 34-21. That's because No. 66 was the hero. Hear! Hear! Late in the third quarter, the 'Skins were ahead 21-14. I recovered a fumble on their 31 and John Unitas took us in. But the point-after kick failed, leaving the 'Skins still ahead. Nifty Norman Snead tried to show his passing stuff. Another interception by No. 66 and a carry back to the Washington 25. John took us in again. Brother Snead was stubborn. He brought his 'Skins back to our nine and uncorked another right into my ever lovin' arms. Clicking like UNIVAC, John took us in for a third TD.

John completed 25 passes that day, a career high mark to date, and threw for four touchdowns to tie another of his personal marks for the eighth time.

R.C. "Kangaroo Kid" Owens, who had been alternating at left offensive end with Raymond Berry, performed the most unique feat of the year by standing under the crossbar and jumping straight up to bat away a certain Washington field goal. The play was so unusual that NFL Commissioner Pete Rozelle called R. C. from San Francisco to get the details.

The Packers clinched the Western Conference title the next day.

Our front office announced the signing of several draft choices, including Bob Vogel from Ohio State (flown to Baltimore by private plane) and Willie Richardson from Jackson State in Mississippi.

We closed the season against the Vikings in Baltimore. The game meant little in the season standings. But it left a few memories.

Late in the first half Bob Boyd fielded a Viking punt, ran first backward, then forward. With Vikings moving in for the kill he flipped the ball to me. Jim Welch moved up alongside to block, but while he was looking for someone to hit, I managed to shove (that's the word for it) the ball into his arms. I knew he was faster — besides that way they would all be chasing him. Jim got to the Viking 23 before being spilled. As I said before, my philosophy is, it's better to be a live chicken than a dead hero.

Jim Parker and Viking tackle Paul Dickson got into a wrestling match which almost turned into a free-for-all. Jim didn't like the way Paul had been treating "his boy" — John Unitas.

Fran Tarkenton was knocked cold, not in the fight, but by a head-on tackle by Wendell Harris. Fran's bad day was partly offset by his teammate Tommy Mason who rushed 143 yards in 20 carries to become the running star of the afternoon.

But the Vikings couldn't handle John Unitas in the fourth quarter when he threw for four touchdown passes, marking the ninth time he had given birth to quads. Raymond Berry caught eight for 131 yards and a touchdown, his first score since the opening game of the season.

The game ended 42-17 with the Baltimore fans singing *Auld Lang Syne* — I think they meant it for Weeb Ewbank whose time, according to the press, was running out.

This same day, Y. A. Tittle broke a record with six touchdown passes in a Giant victory over Dallas. The old veteran of 15

pro years whom we all respected, had played for the Colts in
'48 and '49, then for the 49'ers who traded him to the Giants.
But Yelberton lost the title game to Green Bay 16-7. This brought
the Packers even with us in winning two consecutive titles.

Only Gino Marchetti made All-Pro from our team. Jim Parker
and Bill Pellington made the second team on the All-Pro list.
Bob Boyd, Andy Nelson, and I were "Honorable Mention."

Bravo for the businessmen of Baltimore. The Junior Association of Commerce named me "Baltimore's Man of the Year for
1962." I proudly received the trophy from the Honorable Spiro
T. Agnew, then the County Executive of Baltimore County.

This was also the year our third son was born. Josh Matthew
arrived on October 30. He was our "treat" for Halloween.

Here's how to get your name in the papers.

"V" for victory.

Well, did we win or lose? (Baltimore News-Post photo)

13

"A New Trail Boss"

A coach is hired to be fired. That may sound cruel, but in general that's the way of pro football, except in cases like George Halas where the coach owns the team.

Colts' owner Carroll Rosenbloom called a press conference January 9, 1963, and announced that Don Shula would replace Weeb Ewbank as head football coach. Weeb had piloted the Colts for nine years and developed two championship teams, but the last three seasons had not produced winners. And the Baltimore fans wanted a winner.

Mr. Rosenbloom offered Weeb another job in the organization, but Weeb moved to the New York Jets.

I had known Coach Shula in 1957 when I was the rookie right linebacker and he was the defensive halfback. We had worked together three or four weeks before he moved to the Redskins. Later he went to coach at the Universities of Virginia and Kentucky, then worked for the Detroit Lions, before returning to Baltimore in 1963. Only 33, he had worked under some knowledgable men; Weeb Ewbank at Baltimore; Joe Kuharich at Washington; Blanton Collier at Kentucky; and most recently George Wilson at Detroit. Collier had been the understudy of Cleveland's Paul Brown; Wilson had been one of George Halas' pupils for a dozen years. So Don Shula knew something about the game when he took over the head coaching job in Baltimore. But when asked by a reporter if he felt he was ready for a head coaching job, he replied, "It doesn't matter how I answer that. I'll still have to prove it by winning."

Coaches are people and no two are alike. Weeb Ewbank was the great organizer who always had everything pegged down.

He started every meeting on the split second. He was a regimentarian.

Naturally some thought Shula might have problems coaching old player buddies. Bill Pellington laughed when he heard this and said, " 'Shoes' bossed our whole defense on the field and chewed us out in every game he played."

We found the new coach to be more flexible. He allowed Unitas to be more his own man in calling plays. Having played with some of the older guys seemed to give him more rapport with all of us. Now after six years of playing under Don Shula, I will say that he probably spends more time off the job with his players than any other head coach in pro football. This doesn't mean that he isn't a take-charge man during business hours. He can be as tough as any coach.

Marsha and I paid an early spring visit to the folks in California and almost drowned. We were swimming in about six-and-a-half feet of water when I felt an invisible hand pulling me away from shore — a dreaded rip tide. I saw people ten feet away cavorting out of danger. But I had too much pride to call for help. I thought I could get out by myself and gave it all I had. This almost wasn't enough. I reached shore and flopped on the beach. I had never felt so tired. Marsha's face was white. "Did — did you get in it?" I panted. "Get in what?" she asked. "The rip tide," I answered. Then she said, "I was wondering why that life guard insisted that I grab onto his rope so that he could pull me ashore."

This was the spring I served as lay pastor for a Presbyterian Church in suburban Baltimore. It was also the first time I joined the collegiate Easter rush to Daytona Beach.

Rev. Ed Beck, then an evangelist with the Methodist church and a 6'7" former basketball star at the University of Kentucky, invited me to join his All-American Caravan of Christian Athletes, jazz players, and a minister magician to bring a Christian witness to the students.

What did we do? The jazz band played. Rev. Joe Hale, the magician, left 'em gaping with his sleight of hand stuff. Bill Wade of the Bears and Bill "Crusher" Krisher of the Dallas Texans and

I threw footballs. Chuck Hunter showed them why he was the best college weight lifter in the country.

We headquartered at a motel and put on demonstrations up and down the beach. Everyone wanted to know why we were there. Ed Beck put it this way: "We're here as positive witnesses for our faith in Christ. We are not attempting straight preaching. We want to use elements such as sports and music which students appreciate. We want to share with you what we know about meaningful living." Bill Wade added, "By the grace of God I can throw a football. If I can use that in furthering what Ed and the rest of us are trying to do, then I want to do it." And naturally I got in my two cents. "We are just athletes with faults like everyone else. We are here to help anyone we can help."

Believe me, we had plenty of opportunities to witness. We went where the kids were — on the beach, in motels, and even in bars where I enjoyed my usual "mixed drink" — half orange and half ginger ale. One desire seemed universal among all the kids: Each wanted to get the most out of life. We tried to demonstrate that this could only be accomplished by commitment to Christ and His way of life.

Through Fellowship of Christian Athlete circles Raymond Berry and I learned that Buddy Dial, the star pass receiver of the Pittsburgh Steelers, had started a pre-game team worship service during the past season. The players usually met about nine a.m. in a hotel room for prayers, a brief Bible study, discussion, and occasionally to hear an outside speaker.

Raymond and I talked and prayed about such a service for the Colts. Then I went to Coach Shula, a devout Catholic, who had already asked me to continue leading the team prayers before and after games. I explained that the Catholic boys could attend their services easier than the Protestant boys who had difficulty finding a church of their choosing before the pre-game meal. We wanted a worship service for players and members of the coaching staff who could not easily attend church.

"I'm all for it," Coach Shula said. "I'll even remind the guys during the week not to miss chapel on Sunday."

He was as good as his word and sometimes attended himself.

We had a good turnout of 15-25 players from the start even though it meant getting up a half-hour earlier. Berry and I led most of the services. Our usual format was to open with prayer followed by a Bible reading. Then we would talk about topics that come up in life and read and discuss applicable Bible verses. For example, what is the Christian responsibility in certain situations — like, when a tackler kicks you after the whistle has blown? Or how do you know you're a Christian? (I remember one player responding to this one, "By following the Ten Commandments." I asked him to name six and he could only think of four.) What's the difference between religion and Christianity? Why are you a Christian? And so on.

John Mackey, a halfback from Syracuse and a Colts 1963 draft choice, was one of the rookies who took a strong interest in chapel. John, a Negro, was a Baptist pastor's son from Long Island, New York. He had swept and locked up the church after choir practice and walked little children home after services. At 16, John told his father he was never going to church when he grew up. But later while in college, he noticed on trips home what had happened to some of his old high school buddies who had been left by parents to do as they pleased. Some had gone on dope and had made the police lineup. He began wising up.

"Some of my old buddies," John told us, "tell me I'm lucky now to be playing pro football. Luck isn't it. I followed the rules for right living and didn't cop out as some of them did."

Now for a look at the 1963 Colt football fortunes under our new coach. We started by issuing an ultimatum to the town of Westminister where we trained; the public facilities had to be integrated or else we would train somewhere else. The Baltimore suburb decided that segregation wasn't worth the price of losing the Colts.

We won four out of five of our pre-season games. Tackle Bob Vogel, offensive end John Mackey, the Colts' first and second 1963 draft choices, showed great promise. Free agent Gary Cuozzo also looked good.

Just before the season opener, the *Baltimore News-Post* asked me to divulge some of my secrets of intercepting twenty-four passes in six seasons — a unique record for a linebacker. "I try to make myself scarce when the opposing quarterback is setting up for the snap," I wrote. "If he doesn't know where I am going to be, I've got an important advantage. Whenever possible I keep moving up and down the line behind those big guys up front in hopes that I'll get lost in the crowd. Naturally it also helps to know the passer and receivers. This comes through actual playing experience and also watching game films. Some passers prefer throwing to the sidelines for the important yardage while others will go to the hook-pass or perhaps the quick look-in shot. They're all difficult to defend against but sometimes a guy can get lucky, especially if he's out of the quarterback's range of vision.

"There are other considerations, too, like getting deep fast so as not to be backing up while the throw is being made — or the defender will be off balance when the ball heads in his direction. It also helps to be able to sense the pattern that's developing and go to take the best possible angle to get between the passer and receiver. Anticipation is probably my greatest attribute — this alone can make up for quickness and speed. This is what I call 'football speed' over the 'track man's speed.' "

"But even with all these things going for me they won't avail me anything if I can't hold onto the football. In my first two years in the league I had quite a few knock-downs but only five interceptions. I worked in the 'Raymond Berry net' and caught ball after ball. I realized in a short time the importance of hanging onto the ball."

What happened after the newspaper published this little gem? The Giants came to town for the opener, staked us to a 21-3 lead, then Y. A. Tittle took title to the weak spots in our secondary and whipped us 37-28. Of course, I got no interception — I had given away all my secrets. The Colts did have one excuse! Lenny Moore was hustled off to the hospital just before the game started for an emergency appendectomy. Lenny had been out with injuries during the first six games of the previous season and we had lost four of these.

Don Shula all but cried when the gun sounded ending his first game as the new head coach. He had been given a big build-up in local sports circles. Fan interest was at an all-time high. Tickets were so hard to come by that people had actually been seen scanning the obituary column for the names of season ticket-holders.

The second game looked like a repeat of the first for three quarters as the 49'ers moved ahead 14-10. To make matters worse Raymond Berry suffered a dislocated shoulder and Alex Hawkins, who went in to replace him, was knocked groggy.

Then John Unitas took the offense to a fourth and one situation on the 49'ers one-yard line. He called for Jimmy Orr to take a rollout pass to the right. Jimmy didn't understand the play and went in the opposite direction. Fortunately John spotted him running to the left side of the goal and completed the pass that made the difference between losing or winning.

The next week they could have changed the song to, "Row, row, row your boat, sadly down the stream." We played ball exchange with the Packers 12 times via fumbles and interceptions. Even with Lenny Moore playing a great game, less than three weeks after his appendectomy, the Pack beat us 31-20.

There were some real weirdos in that game. On one, Bart Starr and Tom Moore of the Pack missed connections on a routine handoff. Bart ended up with the ball deep in his own backfield when the ball suddenly dropped from his grasp, hit the ground, and bounced back to him. With Colts closing in, he threw to Boyd Dowler who ran for six points. Is it legitimate to play basketball with a football?

The next game was a toughie. We saw a 3-0 advantage against the Bears disappear in the fourth quarter when relief QB Rudy Bukich flipped a short pass to Ronnie Bull who raced the rest of the way for a touchdown. Our defense had played its heart out and then lost on one perfectly executed play. The one consolation was that I got to see my dad and stepmother after the game.

We yo-yoed through the next seven games, winning and losing until by November 24 we were five and five and out of contention for the Western Conference title.

This was the weekend of national mourning for assassinated President Kennedy. The AFL called off its games. The NFL went ahead and got a pile of criticism. Carroll Rosenbloom, a close friend of the dead president, skipped our game with the Rams and flew to Washington. We lost 17-16 with our Jim Martin missing a short field goal try during the closing minutes. Because of the tragedy, there wouldn't have been much fun even if we had won.

We rose from the ashes to win our last three games. Unitas Airlines seemed to have a franchise in the passing lanes. Against the Redskins John threw for 355 yards and three touchdowns. Against the Vikings he amassed 344 yards in the air and moved beyond his previous season record of 3,099 yards set in 1960. John Mackey looked superhuman in two second-effort scoring plays. Against the Rams in the coldest game I've ever played in Baltimore, John threw to Tom Matte, and wrapped up the game 19-16 with 33 seconds left.

We ended the season 8-6. The Bears and the Giants won conference titles and met for the big game on a cold day in Chicago. I projected the Bears to win 17-14, "if Bill Wade is right." He was, and the Bears took the marbles 14-10.

This was the year John broke Sonny Jurgensen's NFL record with 237 completions. Y. A. Tittle surpassed his own NFL record by passing for 36 touchdowns. And the Cleveland's Jimmy Brown became the first player to gain more than a mile on the ground by rushing for 1,863 yards.

14

"Gladness and Sadness"

Early in 1964 I joined an FCA "team" in Tampa, Florida for four days of spiritual impact. FCA's Bill Krisher, an All-American at the University of Oklahoma and former pro, brought us together from all parts of the country.

Wow! I hadn't seen so many great athletes and coaches assembled in one place since the Giants and the Colts had battled for the NFL title five years before. Since then, in 1969 there were 100 athletes in Dallas, Texas and Knoxville, Tennessee for the same kind of meeting.

Thirty-five of us (if you want to call me a "great" athlete) met at the Causeway Inn to plan the weekend. Football was represented by Bill Wade of the Bears, Tony Romeo of the Patriots, Prentice Gautt of the Cardinals, Maxie Baughan of the Eagles (he later joined the Rams), me, and Coach Tom Landry of Dallas, plus about a dozen All-American college football players. There were enough baseball players to field a team plus the patron saint of the baseball world, 82-year-old Branch Rickey. And there was the one and only Paul Anderson, the strongest man in the world.

Paul is a real "sissy" Christian: 370 pounds, 24-inch neck, 36-inch thighs, and 60-inch chest. An Olympic Gold Medal winner in weight lifting, he holds the record for the most weight ever lifted on the back of any man — 6,270 pounds. That's a couple of pounds more than I can lift.

He puts on weight lifting demonstrations for FCA rallies and other groups. Like setting eight high school boys on a table and shouldering them into the air, then saying, "My strength comes from Christ, and if I can't get through a day without Christ, I know you can't."

Some of us arrived in Tampa before Paul did. I told the guys,

"Well, if Paul doesn't come, *I'll* have to lift the weights."

Fortunately (for me), Paul arrived. With three big speaking and appearance days ahead of us, Bill Krisher organized us into several planning huddles for discussion of what we would say.

Bill asked me to lead one huddle. "Okay, men," I told my group. "Now what will we say to our audiences?"

"People already know about our athletic accomplishments," a baseball player said. "I think we should talk about our moral standards."

Butter-tongued Maxie Baughan spoke up. "We should say more than that."

"I agree, Maxie," I said. "I've been studying the book of Acts recently to learn what the disciples Peter and Paul preached after the crucifixion. I think we should always mention Jesus. He is the Master."

The elderly man with the bushy eyebrows at the end of the table lifted his walking cane and tapped the table for emphasis. We all listened to Branch Rickey, who was Mr. Integrity in the sports world. More than any other man, Branch Rickey had been responsible for integrating professional sports.

"That," he said, "is the red thread of the FCA. I remember once hearing an FCA member tell a sports group in Pittsburgh the advantages of not drinking, not smoking, and not 'running around.' It wasn't enough. I remember that in the old days of the country churches, you stayed around for 'testifying.' There was meat in those testimonies."

After a few more minutes of talking about speech content, I asked, "Now, how are we going to answer questions?"

Maxie Baughan looked back at me. "How do you answer questions, Shinnick?"

"I answer questions from the Bible," I said. "If the answer isn't there, I tell them so and say I am going to give my own opinion. The second thing I tell them is to go directly to God in prayer and find the answer."

"What's an example of a question where you gave your own opinion?" Pitcher Vernon Law wanted to know.

"Well, I've been asked what I thought of Elizabeth Taylor. I said I didn't think she'd make much of a football player."

The orientation gave us all a chance to get better acquainted with the three FCA staff members who were directing the weekend in Tampa.

Bill Krisher told us his way of dealing with opposing linemen who ridiculed his faith. "I kept quiet and hit them as hard as I could. They respect hard tackling." James Jeffrey, the new Executive Director of FCA, and a former football star at Baylor, did a juggling act for us. "There's fewer injuries in this game," he cracked. Loren Young, the FCA director for the Southeast region, a Methodist minister and ex-track coach, entertained us with stories of his visit to Russia. "They've heard about many American athletes," he said. "They know, for example, that Rafer Johnson is a Christian." Loren smiled and added, "You men have a unique opportunity to witness for Christ. You're already committed to athletics. Add to this, commitment to Christ and you've got a tiger in your tank."

We witnessed to a lot of people that weekend. On Friday "Team" members spoke to assemblies in 37 Tampa area schools. Friday evening we hosted a "Professional Baseball" banquet for big league players in the area for spring training. Saturday morning we put on a "Sports Jamboree" at the University of Tampa football field for all county junior and senior high school coaches and athletes. We demonstrated our special skills in weightlifting, football, baseball and basketball. I don't remember what I did — maybe a talkathon.

Saturday afternoon we gave a "Coaches Luncheon" to acquaint the high school coaches with the FCA program. We explained how they could organize FCA huddle groups* in their schools. Saturday night we held a big city-wide public rally. Sunday morning "Team" members spoke in 55 churches during Sunday school and morning worship services. Sunday afternoon we finished with a fellowship luncheon for the visiting "Team" members and the local committee.

*For information on the current FCA program and instructions on how to start an FCA huddle/fellowship in a high school or college, write the Fellowship of Christian Athletes, 812 Traders National Bank Building, 1125 Grand Avenue, Kansas City, Missouri.

It was one of the greatest three days of my life. I came home convinced that FCA had big things ahead.

Don Shula was still in the honeymoon stage with the Baltimore fans. He felt we could win the Western Conference, although the experts gave the nod to Green Bay. He bought Lou Michaels from the Steelers to give more depth in the kicking department and Steve Stonebreaker from the Vikings to help with linebacking.

Lou didn't know how to take me the first day he came out for a drill. I saw him standing a little ways off from the huddle. ("I didn't want to be pushy," he said later.) I grabbed him and yelled, "Okay, rookie, get in the huddle and learn something." The guys roared, but poor Lou who had been in the pros only one year less than I had been, was embarrassed.

"Stony" Stonebreaker almost split his sides the day he stood in line waiting for his name to be called as players were introduced for the Colt inter-squad game in the stadium. I walked over to him and said in a serious tone, "Don't feel bad if the fans boo you, 'Stoney.' There'll be a tremendous cheer when I'm introduced. That's cause they love me in Baltimore and they know you're trying to steal my job." I think "Stoney" took me seriously because when his name was called, he moved like a tortoise. He didn't get my job, either.

With the Colts, you have to learn to take a joke as well as tell one. Once at a luncheon with Gino Marchetti I said, "I don't understand why the Colts have never given me a game ball." Marchetti, who had always had the job of polling the players after a game to select the player they felt most deserving of the game ball, piped up. "Shinnick, in all the years I've been asking, your name has been mentioned just once." He paused, then added, "By you." The crowd roared and I laughed with them.

Seriously, I think that's one reason why the Colts have such great team spirit. We've learned to laugh at and with one another.

But we didn't do any laughing after the Vikings shot us down 34-24 in the first game of the season. We rushed four men most of the time, a mistake against a scrambler like Fran Tarkenton. I was benched for the first time in my professional career. Our dressing room in Minneapolis was as quiet as King Tut's tomb when I led the guys in the after-game prayer.

All the following week we talked about little else except how we would beat the Packers. Before the game, Gino Marchetti asked the coaches to leave and gave us a little pep talk. "Tarkenton and the Vikings embarrassed us," he said. "We can't afford to be humiliated like that again." The message got through.

For the second time, I sat on the bench and watched our defense take the field. In my right linebacking position was Jackie Burkett, a reserve player from Auburn. Remembering my shoddy performance against the Vikings, I made no beef.

I was still on the sidelines when the Colts led 21-13. Paul Hornung had missed his first extra-point kick, in 152 attempts.

I watched my replacement, Burkett, slam head-on into Jim Taylor, then get up with difficulty. He had to be helped off the field. Don Shula slapped my back and said, "Go in."

The Pack picked up another touchdown in the third quarter on Jim Taylor's 23-yard run. Hornung kicked a bull's-eye this time, bringing his team to within one point of us.

With about a minute left to play, the score still stood 21-20, but the Pack was at our 31. We all knew Hornung was itching to kick a field goal if they couldn't make a first down or score a touchdown.

Bart Starr called the play. Three or four seconds later I saw the ball wobbling through the air. Anytime I see a ball not spiralling smoothly, I know someone up front has put on a tremendous rush. The ball wobbled, and dropped like a wounded dove into my arms. I hugged it to my chest and sat down. There was no reason to risk a fumble by trying to run it back. The offense then came in and ran the clock out to preserve the one-point win.

Talk about jubilation. In one week we had come from the bottom of the well to the moon. Every man among us felt we could go all the way after beating the Packers.

We were in the Milky Way when the Bears came to Baltimore for our first game before the home folks. We had whipped the Packers — the team picked to win in 1964. Now we wanted to take the team that had won the title in 1963. Also, we remembered the 57-0 humiliation the Bears had dished out to us two years before.

We made Halas' men look like stuffed teddy bears as we beat them 52-0. Papa Bear summed up after the game, "We were stinko!" Coach Shula substituted freely, even putting in the temperamental rookie Joe Don Looney in the fourth quarter. Looney came out as the Colts' top rusher with 82 yards in eight carries and one touchdown. There was one crazy incident where Mike Ditka fumbled, and I tried to pick it up. Mike kicked it out of bounds and the officials ruled it a deliberate kick.

The next week we climbed on top of the division ladder by dumping the Rams 35-20. Jimmy Orr carried in three touchdown passes and Bob Boyd made a key interception.

Next we defeathered the Cardinals 47-27; no one had scored this many against the Cards since they had moved to St. Louis in 1960. Lou Michaels booted four field goals and five extra points. "You're looking better all the time, Rookie," I told him after the game. He laughed. The afternoon before the evening game, the baseball Cards beat the Yankees 5-2 in the fifth game of the World Series.

Roll, Colts, roll!

Well, we didn't exactly roll over Green Bay in our second meeting of the year. We beat the Pack 24-21 on Lenny Moore's super-duper five-yard fight to the goal line with a minute and eight seconds to play. Hornung was the goat again. He missed four field goal tries and had another blocked.

Colts 34—Lions 0. How about that! Now we had won five straight since my game-saving interception in Green Bay and had matched our longest winning streak in history. Lenny Moore set a new NFL mark by scoring overland in nine straight contests.

We earned our seventh consecutive win by a gallop of 37-7 over the 49'ers. Raymond Berry moved past Don Hutson on his way to catch Bill Howton as pro football's top receiver. He got the game ball. Steve Stonebreaker grabbed a bad 49'er pass from center and rambled in for his first pro touchdown.

We had eight in a row with a 40-24 romp over the Bears. Rookie Tony Lorick got the game ball for rushing 14 times for 126 yards. Defensive safety Jimmy Welch made the hardest tackle when he slammed into the goal post while pursuing Mike Ditka. He actually thought he had hit big Mike.

Now who else should appear from the far north but the Minnesota Vikings? And they didn't bring a bag of presents for us. We had seen these guys before and marched out to avenge our opening loss of the season.

These pests were brash enough to lead us 14-10 in the fourth quarter. But old Mr. Clutch himself, John Unitas, tricked them out on a fourth down with seven yards to go. The Vikes were expecting a short pass when John heaved the ball behind the line of scrimmage to Lenny Moore who poured through for eleven yards. Two plays later, John threw to Alex Hawkins in the end zone for the final touchdown. And that was the old ball game.

After the game, Vikings coach Norm Van Brocklin heard that Gino Marchetti was due to retire at the end of the season. "If he retires," Dutch declared, "I'll send him a gift."

One more victory and we could clinch the Western Conference title.

The Rams were our victims 24-7. Gino Marchetti led the assault that tossed the Ram field generals back 11 times for 102 yards.

After the game we drank pop and had a shower party, soaking Carroll Rosenbloom, Don Shula, and the assistant coaches.

Now that we had clinched the conference, any other season wins would be icing on the cake.

Apparently we didn't want the icing very badly. We won our eleventh game in a row over the 49'ers in a lackluster contest that isn't worth remembering. The 49'ers did everything but walk off the field, giving up five interceptions and three fumbles. We scored only one touchdown. Neither offense was up to regular season performance.

Humpty Dumpty had a little fall. The Lions stopped our winning streak, but it didn't affect our conference lead. The Cleveland Browns clinched the Eastern Conference title.

Naturally the press jumped on us, suggesting that if we didn't come alive we might end up losing the title match.

The barbs must have hurt. We came back and closed the season with a 45-17 win over the Redskins. Raymond Berry reached an all-time high in career receptions with 502. Lenny Moore scored twice and broke Packer Jim Taylor's mark of 19 touchdowns in a season.

Old pros Gino Marchetti and Bill Pellington (24 years of service between them) were honored in retirement ceremonies. They got enough gifts to open a department store. "I think I'll retire," I said — but not loud enough for Don Shula to hear.

We spent the next two weeks getting ready for the title game against the Browns. The sports world buzzed at the prospects of a match between the "Wing" (John Unitas) and the "Legs" (Jimmy Brown). Both men were tops in their departments.

Colt fans descended on Cleveland in force. The day before the game Jimmy Brown went into the Pick Carter Hotel drug store and sat down to listen to the juke box. Suddenly a mob of Colt fans, accompanied by a bugler, came parading toward him chanting "C-O-L-T-S . . ." He fled. More Colt fans camped in the lobby of the hotel. They cheered for the Colts and razzed the Brown players as they passed through. If the Browns got any sleep that night, it wasn't the fault of the people from Baltimore.

The 1964 title game was one I'd like to forget. Our defense got pummelled. John Wooten, a 255-pounder, hit me so hard once, I thought both legs were broken. Our offense couldn't have scored with rockets. Gary Collins took in three scoring passes (and won the sports car as the game's most outstanding player) and Jimmy Brown rushed for 114 yards. The debacle ended 27-0. I grabbed off the only Colt interception of the day.

Our loser's share amounted to about $5,000 per man, but we didn't brag about the money. About the only good feeling I had was when Don Shula, the NFL's "Coach of the Year," said my pass interception in the second game of the season against Green Bay had ignited the 11-game winning streak. But, sob, why couldn't one of those wins have been against Cleveland?

Sure, we had won more games than Cleveland in 1964. But in the NFL you can win the most games and still lose the big crown. It's the title game that really counts.

Here's Johnny, and I don't mean Carson.

Two members of Shinnick's All-Time NFL Team. At left is ole' buddy Raymond Berry, five times All-Pro, sometimes called "Mr. Gluefingers."

Below is Lenny Moore. I never saw anyone who could catch "Sputnik" after he broke loose with the ball.

Zeroing in on "Brother" Fran Tarkenton.

Max Magee seems a little upset. (Baltimore News-Post photo)

"Come to Papa!"

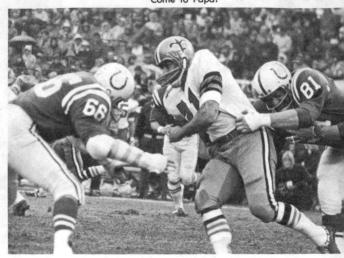

Lion taming.

Gino "the Giant" Marchetti made a lot of quarterbacks sleep easier when he retired. He's without doubt the greatest pass rusher the game has ever known.

Earl Morrall quarterbacked the Colts to the NFL championship in 1968. I've known Earl since college days when he directed the Michigan State attack against UCLA in the 1956 Rose Bowl.

These are not the "flying horsemen" — just four of the Colt players who are active with me in the Fellowship of Christian Athletes: Bob Vogel, No. 72; John Mackey, No. 88; Bill Curry, No. 50; and Bob Boyd, No. 40. Try telling these guys that Christianity is only for sissies.

COLTS HEAD COACH DON SHULA

MEMBERS OF THE 1968 NFL
CHAMPIONSHIP SQUAD

TOP ROW (left to right): (79) Lou Michaels, (76) Fred Miller, (49) David Lee, (75) John Williams, (73) Sam Ball, (78) Bubba Smith, (72) Bob Vogel, (85) Roy Hilton, (81) Ordell Braase, (52) Dick Szymanski.

SECOND ROW (left to right): Offensive Backfield Coach Don McCafferty, Defensive Backfield Coach Chuck Moll, (62) Glenn Ressler, (71) Dan Sullivan, (74) Billy Ray Smith, (61) Cornelius Johnson, (55) Ron Porter, (88) John Mackey, (50) Bill Curry, (53) Dennis Gaubatz, (87) Willie Richardson, (84) Tom Mitchell, Head Coach Don Shula, Offensive Line Coach John Sandusky.

THIRD ROW (left to right): (51) Bob Grant, (28) Jimmy Orr, (2) Timmy Brown, (32) Mile Curtis, (19) John Unitas, (43) Lenny Lyles, (45) Jerry Hill, (40) Bob Boyd, (15) Earl Morrall, (66) Don Shinnick.

BOTTOM ROW (left to right): (27) Ray Perkins, (41) Tom Matte, (16) Jim Ward, (26) Preston Pearson, (25) Alex Hawkins, (34) Terry Cole, (20) Jerry Logan, (37) Ocie Austin, (21) Rick Volk, (47) Charlie Stukes.

NOT SHOWN: Defense Line Coach Bill Arnsparger, Assistant Trainer Dick Spassoff, End Coach Dick Bielski, Assistant Trainer John Spassoff, Equipment Manager Fred Schubach, Head Trainer Eddie Block.

This is not what I do during off season. (Baltimore News-Post photo)

As I said to the New York Jets' offense, "Verrrry interesting." (U.S. Army photo)

15

"One Bad Call"

I followed the call of the waves and went back to Daytona Beach for the third straight spring. "This is getting to be a habit," I told Bill Wade.

We operated about the same as we had the past two years: the jazz band played, we athletes pitched balls around, and Joe Hale did magic tricks. The added big plus was strong man Paul Anderson who had been with us at Tampa the year before. Believe me, no one kicked sand in this guy's face! He lifted six college boys on a platform and said, "It takes a man to follow Christ."

One evening Wade, Joe Hale, Paul Anderson, and I went into a night club. We had made arrangements with the manager ahead of time to put on a program. When the emcee announced us, everything stopped — even the go-go girls sat down in their cages. It was quieter than a Sunday school class for half an hour while we gave our testimonies for Christ. After our "show," a guy came up to me and said, "I wish I had the guff to do what you fellows are doing."

Another evening a fellow invited me to a party in a motel room where whisky and beer bottles were lined against the wall and three couples were in bed. It was an "anything goes" situation.

The kids always seemed eager to talk about sex, although I doubt if all students who go to the beaches during Easter week have illicit sex. Plenty do, I'm sure. Their general philosophy seemed to be, "Eat, drink, and enjoy yourself for tomorrow you may get drafted, die in a nuclear war, or get lost in the middle-class society."

Loren Young, the Southeast Director of the FCA, was with us. One afternoon he spotted a guy wearing a sweater lettered:

STAMP OUT VIRGINITY. Loren, the soft-spoken southern gentle-man type, stopped the boy and said, "Virginia — did you go to school there? Uh, no, it says virginity. Hey, that's a neat sweater. You ought to keep it and take good care of it until you have a grown-up daughter. Then you could give it to the first fellow who takes her out."

The guy's face turned chalk white and he went away. But later that day he sought out Loren and said, "I won't wear that sweater again. You really taught me something."

After Easter I continued speaking about four times a week. Then our fourth son was born on May 15th, my 30th birthday. We named him Peter, because we liked the name so much.

In June I went to the Fellowship of Christian Athletes con-ference at Black Mountain, North Carolina. This was one of six summer conferences across the nation* where FCA staff members and pro athletes directed programs for high school and college boys.

Each day was packed with inspiration, perspiration, and fun. After breakfast came personal devotions, then a morning as-sembly followed by "huddle" sessions where the high school and college kids got acquainted with the faculty.

We encouraged the kids to open up and talk freely about the key concerns of life, their most important interests in life — faith, morality, goals, family, etc. We huddle leaders then made our-selves available for private talks.

One college freshman said he wanted to hear my definition of what a Christian is. What he really wanted was to defend his way of having fun. "I go out and shack up with a couple of girls at night and forget about it the next day," he said.

"So what," I replied. "What kind of fun is that?"

"I'm having fun in bed."

"But how long does it last? What happens afterward?" I

---

*FCA now operates 15 summer conferences for high school and college athletes at various locations across the nation. Enrollment in-formation may be obtained by writing the Fellowship of Christian Athletes, 1125 Grand Avenue, Kansas City, Missouri 64106.

countered. Finally we got down to a frank discussion about life and what it means to follow Christ.

Another high school fellow sought out Fran Tarkenton, an alumnus of the school he attended. This boy, Pat Hodgson, a top football player at the University of Georgia, later told what happened: "Fran and I walked away from a group discussion and I started talking to him about my life. It really hurt as I told him some things about myself. He listened and seemed to understand. Then we knelt down beside a wall and Fran prayed with me and for me. That was the night when Christ forgave my past sins and came into my life. I've never been the same since."* Pat later went to play for the Washington Redskins and became a leader in FCA.

A big feature of the conference was the "Dogpatch Olympics" where the guys played volley ball, basketball, and touch football with the pros. Then in the evening we had a worship service with an appeal for commitment. Many of my good friends who are outstanding athletes date the turning point of their lives to these services.

For example, Fran Tarkenton, says, "The great turning point for me came at the Fellowship of Christian Athletes Conference in Estes Park, Colorado, back in 1958. There I heard some of my boyhood heroes speak unashamedly about their Christian faith. Men like Otto Graham and Donn Moomaw really impressed me. I knew they had come long distances just to attend the conference and share their faith in Christ.

"At Estes Park I became aware of my weak and ineffectual Christian witness. I realized that I hadn't surrendered all phases of my life to God's will. I told God that I would give Him my life completely — with no reservations attached. I would go anywhere, do anything as He gave me strength and guidance."

Dr. Billy Graham spoke at Black Mountain during the 1965 conference. When I was introduced to him, I said, "Dr. Who?" One afternoon Dr. Graham and his associate T. W. Wilson, James Jeffrey, the Executive Director of FCA, and I played a

---

*The Will to Win, p. 81, Zondervan Publishing House.

round of golf. At the third hole, I missed a close putt. Dr. Graham jumped about three feet in the air. As we moved off the green, I said to Jeffrey, "Man, I'm glad I missed that putt. I think if I had made it, I would have been the first man to cause Billy Graham to swear. He really gets excited about his golf."

A few weeks later race riots erupted in Cambridge, Maryland. Raymond Berry, Jim Parker, and I went down to speak at a previously scheduled athletic rally. I told Jim, a Negro, "If the whites come after us, you hide behind me. If the blacks come, I'll hide behind you." I don't remember what Raymond said — probably, "Where does that leave me?"

Football time came around again and there was some speculation that I might be moved out of my starting position by fresh competition. But I brought my weight down from 240 to 225 and gave training camp and the exhibitions all I had. When we opened against the troublesome Vikings on September 20 I was in the starting lineup for the ninth straight year. Except for Gino Marchetti and Bill Pellington who had retired, we had about the same faces in the starting offensive and defense, as we had the year before. Mike Curtis, a promising rookie linebacker and full-back from Duke, was one who almost knocked off a starting position.

It hadn't been so hot in Baltimore since 1896. They said the temperature was 94 in the stands, but it was at least 120 on the field — at least I felt that hot. I mention the heat to point out the Vikings' mistake. They were drinking water on the side lines. I believe they got water-logged. They poured it on us for the first quarter and actually led 10-0 even though Bob Boyd's pass steal snapped Fran's string of 76 passing attempts without an interception. Then the boys from Minnesota began to wilt and our offense began tightening the noose. The game ended 35-16. Berry and Orr made fine catches. John Mackey looked better than ever. Lenny Moore extended his scoring streak to 18 straight games. I think the Vikes learned a lesson in moderation that day.

Green Bay was next on our agenda. Tex Maule, *Sport Illustrated*'s fount of all football knowledge, had forecast before the season that we would finish behind the Packers in the Western Conference. We wanted to prove him wrong.

Ha! We gave the game away. With Starr, Taylor, and Hornung injured, the Pack still beat us 20-17. Five Colt fumbles and two interceptions were too much. The Pack can thank old horse thief Herb Adderly for the victory. He grabbed up two passes that accounted for 77 yards and 10 points. Then he swiped Tom Matte's fumble in the last minute when the Colts had a chance to tie or win. It was Adderly who addled us.

We played turn about and took the 49'ers by 3 points the following week. The difference came from a San Francisco gamble on the opening kickoff. They goofed on an onside kickoff and our Lou Michaels punched through a field goal. The same day the Bears' sensational new rookie Gale Sayers ran for two touchdowns against Green Bay. However, Green Bay got the victory which made them 3 and 0, and tied with the Lions who were also undefeated. Over in the other conference, the Cleveland Browns continued in the lead. In a 35-17 win over Philadelphia, the Browns' Jimmy Brown passed Don Hutson's career touchdown record of 105 to set a new NFL mark. And in the other league, the rookie Joe Namath began showing that he might be worth all the gold the Jets had dished out to get him.

The next week we pulled the Lions down into second place (behind the Packers who beat the 49'ers) with a 31-7 rout. Unitas-to-Orr was the magic combination that put the points on the scoreboard. It was Joe Don Looney's birthday (the Colts had traded him to the Lions) and he celebrated it by making the Lions' lone touchdown. Later the Lions' passed Joe Don over to the Redskins.

We kept on winning.

Colts 38 — Redskins 7. The Washington fans booed both us and their coach Bill McPeak. One banner read: COLOR MCPEAK GONE. McPeak charged us Colt linebackers with being poor sports by calling out "hut" in the same cadence Sonny Jurgensen was using. The Pack won over Detroit and kept a game ahead of us.

Colts 35 — Rams 20. Unitas dehorned Los Angeles with three

last-quarter touchdowns. But the Pack beat Dallas and kept their one game margin.

Happy Halloween! We beat the 49'ers 34-28 and Gale Sayers and company crushed the Packers 31-10. Our win and the Green Bay loss put us in a tie for first place. For the second week in a row, Unitas came from behind to take the Colts off the hook. But the big bad Bears were next.

Hey! Hey! Our defense held Gale Sayers, alias the Kansas Comet, to 17 yards rushing, and even with Unitas getting knocked out in the third quarter, we bopped the Bears 26-21. I made a key interception on the Colt 6 in the first quarter, but later broke my forearm hitting Jon Arnett's helmet. The Colts put me on their injured reserve list, thus requiring me to miss four games — the only league games I've ever missed.

Gary Cuozzo had to replace Unitas in the third quarter when the toast of Baltimore was taken out with a bruised back. They're still arguing in Chicago about Cuozzo's clinching touchdown throw to Raymond Berry. Berry got the ball as he crossed the goal line, then had it knocked out of his hand by Dave Whitsell. Raymond himself admitted that had he lost the same ball anywhere but behind the goal line, it would have been a fumble. The Bears argued he wasn't over the goal line when Whitsell knocked the ball from him.

Afterward, Raymond told reporters, "I honestly don't know. I wouldn't have kicked if the officials had called it incomplete. But the official was in a much better position to see and call the play than I was." Raymond's honesty shook some people up, but he was right. You can't always be precise about a close play. The official must make a judgment call. Sure, computers and electronics could be more accurate. But I (and I think other players feel the same way) wouldn't want the game turned over to machines. If we did, we might as well be at the race track. Let the officials continue to make their judgment calls. The arguments add to the color of the game.

Lest I forget, the Lions stopped the Packers, putting us all alone at the head of the Western Conference. I wondered if Tex Maule might not be mulling over his pre-season prediction.

One additional note. The morning before the game, a friend

was driving Unitas to Catholic Mass when a policeman stopped their car and pushed a paper toward John. "How about autographing this for my boy?" he asked.

Great as John is, the next game showed we could win without him as Cuozzo called the signals for a 42-21 win over the Vikings. Green Bay edged Los Angeles 6-3 and stayed one game back of us. It sure felt better to be a game ahead of the Pack instead of a game behind as we had been earlier in the season.

What a game we had with the Eagles. With Norm Snead and pals behind only three points, Bobby Boyd pulled Snead's pass right out of Raymond Poage's chest in the end zone and got a standing ovation. The play was similar to the one in which Berry and Whitsell had figured in Chicago. With Unitas back in the quarterback slot we won 34-24. Jimmy Orr zipped to the hospital for X-rays and a shot of pain-killer for a shoulder injury, then returned in time to catch the clinching touchdown.

Green Bay stayed on our heels by beating Minnesota. We had four games to go.

Detroit tied us 24-24 in the first of the four. But Green Bay lost to the Rams and dropped a game and a half below us.

The real tragedy came the next week when the Bears blanked us 13-0 and knocked Unitas out for the season with a knee injury.

Green Bay's win over the Vikings shaved our lead to one-half game. Oh, brother!

We figured our next week's game with Green Bay would be the big one. It was — for the Pack. Hornung stung us with five touchdowns. Final score 42-27. Cuozzo suffered a shoulder separation. I should mention that I was back at my old linebacking position wearing an arm cast. Apparently the Pack didn't catch my number or they would have been scared to death.

Now the Pack was a half game ahead of us and both of us had one more game to go. We only had Tom Matte, a converted halfback to call the signals.

On Thursday night before our Saturday afternoon game with the Rams, the Colts got a quarterback in trade, Ed Brown from the Steelers. Matte and Brown both played against L.A. with Coach Shula calling most of the plays for them. Matte with his high, squeaky voice had players on both sides in stitches when he called signals. But Tom did an amazing job. Rolling out and running on designed patterns, he gained 99 yards in 16 carries. Everyone blocked. Ed Brown threw for one very important touchdown. On the defense we gave it all we had and when the gun sounded we were ahead 20-17.

Whew! What an escape. Now if the 49'ers could beat the Packers on Sunday, we would win the Western Conference. In case of a tie, there would be a playoff.

Back in Baltimore we watched the game on TV. At the start I toasted the 49'ers with potato salad; when Vern Burke caught the tying touchdown pass for the 49'ers, I ran up and kissed his image on the screen. The game ended 24-24.

The play-off for the conference title was held on a cold afternoon in Green Bay the day after Christmas. The press experts couldn't see how we could win without a quarterback. Unitas and Cuozzo were still out with injuries. My arm was still in a cast from the fracture given by the Bears back on November 7. But pride and determination to do our best pushed us to give everything we had. Perhaps it isn't fair to compare games, but we may have been higher for this one than any game during the past eight years, including the 1958 title game. In my mind, this was the second best football game ever played.

The play for which I will probably be most remembered by Baltimore fans came just after the opening kickoff. Starr hit Bill Anderson for a ten-yard gain. Lenny Lyles hit Anderson so hard he fumbled. I pounced on the ball with my one good arm — and began running for the end zone. Starr started for me, but Jimmy Welch took care of him with a block hard enough to put the Green Bay quarterback out of action for the day.

Incredible! Here we were ahead 6-0 and I had the first touchdown of my pro career.

With Matte calling signals in his high-pitched voice, we got three more points and led 10-0 at the half. Tom ran a ball control, ground-hugging offense most of the time. He passed only twelve times, completing five. He never lost the ball.

Zeke Bratkowski, playing for Starr, moved the Packers to our one in the third quarter, then Hornung hit off right guard for a touchdown. The score stayed 10-7 until late in the fourth when two official calls went against us. The first, a 15-yard personal foul penalty, was called when Billy Ray Smith downed Zeke with a chop on his helmet with a swinging forearm. We couldn't understand that call since Zeke had the ball. The call nullified an 8-yard loss and gave Green Bay a 15-yard-advance to our 43.

From there the Packers moved to field goal range with Chandler kicking high from the 22. The official signalled three points, but the film showed the ball had gone *a yard outside the goal post.* The next year they extended the goal post ten feet higher for some reason — maybe because of this call; I don't know. I don't say the official deliberately called in favor of Green Bay. I only say he used poor judgment.

The "field goal" tied us 10-10 and the game went into sudden death. After about 13 minutes of see-saw play, Chandler kicked for the three points that won for Green Bay.

Seven hundred die-hard fans met us at the Baltimore airport. They lifted Matte to their shoulders and shouted, 'You're still No. 1 with us."

But the cheers couldn't erase the fact that we had lost. "We lost," Bobby Boyd said. "That's all that matters. I'd rather get beat 503 to 0 than this way."

Green Bay moved on to down Cleveland 23-12 for the NFL title with Chandler kicking three field goals. This game meant nothing to us.

We went against the Dallas Cowboys, runners-up in the Eastern Conference, in the Play-off Bowl in Miami. Our "imposter" quarterback, Tom Matte, gave the Cowboys something to talk about by engineering a 35-3 rout. The Dallas offense leaked like a sieve. Their pass pocket had more holes than the pockets of a skid row bum. I think the Cowboys were impatient to get back to the swimming pool.

So ended another year via Route 66.

16

"Foiled Again . . . and Again"

A balmy spring helped me forget the day in Green Bay when we lost the Western Conference championship and perhaps the NFL title by a bad call. Instead of going to Daytona Beach for the Easter rush, Raymond Berry and I went to Jamaica, Puerto Rico, and the Bahamas and helped a minister with special services.

A few weeks later five of us — Raymond Berry, Willie Richardson, Bobby Boyd, Bob Vogel, and I — went to the FCA conferences. Vogel and I took our families to Black Mountain, North Carolina. Frank Broyles (U. of Arkansas), Bob Timberlake (Giants), Jerry Stovall (football Cardinals), Tom Landry (Cowboys), Fran Tarkenton (Giants), and Paul Anderson brought some great evening messages.

We came back to Baltimore steamed up to do more for Christ within the ranks of FCA. Bob and Andrea Vogel, who had made commitments to Christ at Black Mountain, suggested we start a Friday night Bible study for players and their wives.

This turned out to be a great idea. We started the first Friday night of the season and continued through December. About eight or nine couples came out each week to read and discuss a passage of Scripture, talk about life situations, pray informally, and enjoy refreshments together. And the gals got together by themselves for their own once-a-week Bible study.

Right after the FCA Black Mountain camp, the NFL and AFL announced a merger agreement intended to lead to full integration with 28 teams for the 1970 season. The merger called for a unified draft and an interleague "Super Bowl" between the winners of both leagues. I was glad to see this come. Not that I thought that the AFL was equal to the NFL — but I felt that the money war over top college players was not healthy for pro football.

Along with the merger announcements, the NFL office stated that in 1967 its 16 teams (including the new franchise in New Orleans) would divide into four divisions with divisional leaders playing for conference titles, conference winners playing for the NFL title, and the NFL title-holder playing the AFL champ in the Super Bowl.

It came to be that time again. There was speculation that Mike Curtis or some other player might replace me in the starting right linebacker position. But when the season opened, I was back in my old spot along with Steve Stonebreaker at left and Dennis Gaubatz holding down the middle. "Shinnick," said a writer, "is what Jim Gilliam was for years to the Dodgers. He's always going, never gone."

Stoney, Dennis, and I had learned to work together. Stoney covered the wide flare passes; Denny the close flare passes, and I — well, sometimes I just took off and followed my hunch. One writer accused me of being "always out of position." There might be some truth in that, but my thirty pass interceptions to date (more than any other linebacker) stood for something.

We lost the opener 24-3 to the Packers. Our offense couldn't have scored that day on a moving sidewalk, maybe because Unitas was rusty. Then we beat the Vikings 38-23 and the 49'ers 36-14 (Lou Michaels kicked five field goals to tie an NFL record) before moving to Chicago for a romp over the Bears. At this time we were tied for second in the conference with the Rams and Detroit. Naturally, the Packers were first with a 3-0 record.

The Bears whomped us 27-17 and I didn't get to settle the score for my broken arm. The Orioles did a lot better, wiping out the Dodgers four games to none in the World Series. As the Colts' "baseball authority" (Bob Boyd, Lou Michaels and our equipment manager, Fred Schubach would argue that), I had said the Orioles would have to beat Sandy Koufax which they did.

We bombed the Lions 45-14, then squeaked past the Vikings (and back into second place) 20-17 in the closing seconds. The Vikings pulled off one of their typically unpredictable plays.

Fran handed the ball off to his fullback, Bill Brown, who whirled and lateralled the ball back to Fran. While we were watching these fancy-prancy maneuvers, Paul Flatley got behind us and caught a 41-yard pass. The flea-flicker fooled us again.

Before the Viking game, Don Shula told us to quit thinking about the undefeated Packers and concentrate on winning a game at a time. "We can't do anything about Green Bay until we play them again," he said. That wouldn't come for seven weeks.

His talk must have done some good, because we won five of our next six games. We could have lost to the surprising Falcons, the newest NFL franchise. Randy Johnson actually completed more passes than John Unitas. The Falcons intercepted two of John's passes and ran up more first downs than the Colts. Our offense found out that Tommy Nobis, the Falcons' first draft choice, was as good as his press clippings. But our defense grabbed five Falcon passes (I got a couple) which helped give us the 19-7 win.

December 10, a Saturday when we played Green Bay, was another day I'll never forget. We had lost three games and were a game behind the conference-leading Packers who had lost two. If we could win this one, we would be tied for the lead with only one game remaining.

Except for two crucial plays, we certainly would have won. On the last play of the first period John Mackey took a 31-yard pass from Unitas near the goal line. Mackey stumbled backward and fell into the end zone. Along the way he dropped the football and the officials claimed he didn't have possession past the goal line. Like the 1965 Unitas-to-Berry touchdown in Chicago (called in our favor), this was a judgment call. Unitas insisted that Mackey had possession inside the goal, but the officials made the decision and we failed to get the big points.

Then with just over a minute remaining in the game, and with the Packers leading 14-10, Unitas fumbled at the Green Bay 15. *Sports Illustrated* called this "a million dollar fumble," meaning that if the Colts had won and gone on to take the championship, we would have picked up the million which the Packers received.

The Packers beat Dallas for the NFL title, then proved the superiority of the NFL over the AFL by taking Kansas City 35-10 in the Super Bowl. Each Packer player's share amounted to about $25,000.

It isn't worth mentioning, but I will say that we lost our last game of the season to the 49'ers. This gave us a 9-5 record, second behind the Packers. Then we beat the Eagles in the Play-off Bowl, but who cares about that? We lost $25,000 apiece during that December 10th game with Green Bay. Had we won, I'm certain we would have gone all the way.

The next year, the NFL was reorganized into four divisions of four teams each, with each team playing most of its games against division opponents, and play-offs between the division winners scheduled to determine the Conference champs. This was the lineup:

WESTERN CONFERENCE

Coastal Division	Central Division
Baltimore Colts	Chicago Bears
Los Angeles Rams	Detroit Lions
San Francisco 49'ers	Green Bay Packers
Atlanta Falcons	Minnesota Vikings

EASTERN CONFERENCE

Century Division	Capital Division
Cleveland Browns	Dallas Cowboys
New York Giants	Philadelphia Eagles
Pittsburgh Steelers	Washington Redskins
St. Louis Cardinals	New Orleans Saints
	(new club)

The new New Orleans Saints stocked their club by selecting 42 "unprotected" veterans from the 14 older clubs. The one-year-old Atlanta Falcons were exempted from this draft. The Saints took three linebackers from the Colts, leaving only me, Dennis Gaubatz, Mike Curtis, and rookie Barry Brown. This practically guaranteed that I would continue to be a starter, but it hurt us in depth. I was sort of proud that the Colts had "protected" me through the formation of four new clubs.

After the Saints stocked their 42, the trading began. The

Colts traded Gary Cuozzo for the Saints' first draft choice, big Bubba Smith. We also picked up Bill Curry (whom the Saints had taken from Green Bay in their new club draft) to back up Dick Szymanski at center. Bill, a fine Christian, strengthened our FCA cadre at Baltimore. And we received Alabama's Ray Perkins and Rich Volk in the college draft. Bubba looked like another Gino Marchetti in the defensive line and Perkins showed potential for becoming another Raymond Berry.

But the Colts for the most part continued to be a veteran squad. This year, the experts predicted that we could win it all if Unitas could stay healthy and have one of his better years.

We started the new alignment by playing the surprisingly strong Falcons. They looked like patsies in the first half as we ran up a 31-7 lead. Then Randy Johnson came to life and scored 24 points. Only Tom Matte's fourth quarter run saved us from a tie, although John Unitas passed for 401 yards and broke his own club record of 397 yards set against Cleveland back in 1959.

Jimmy Orr dislocated his shoulder in the Falcon game and stayed out the whole season. The next week, against the Eagles, Willie Richardson started in his place and made eleven catches for two touchdowns. Actually the Eagles game was closer than the 38-6 score indicated. We were leading 14-6 in the third quarter and they were headed for our goal line when I intercepted Norm Snead's pass. It was my second interception for the day and ran my career lifetime total of interceptions to 35. The Associated Press named me "Defensive Player of the Week," the second time I had been so honored since coming into the pros.

After the game NFL publicity man Don Weiss asked me why I hadn't tried to run back either interception. "A linebacker isn't trained to run with the ball," I said. "He barely has time on the practice field to practice catching the ball, much less run with it. How many times have you seen a linebacker intercept a pass, run a few yards, get hit, and fumble the ball back to the other team? If I coach when I'm through playing, I'm going to tell my linebackers to fall down or run out of bounds after they get an interception."

We romped over the 49'ers 41-7, then beat the Bears to bring our record to four wins without a loss. Ray Perkins, in only his second appearance, caught five passes against the 49'ers for 110 yards and two touchdowns. Ray was beginning to look more and more like the successor to Raymond Berry. And Unitas, the best known of the eleven over-30 Colt starters, could win according to 49'ers coach Jack Christiansen "with nine or ten girls on his offense." But John never made that claim.

Next came the Rams who were a game behind us in the Western Conference. In the past the Packers had been the bone in our throat. After this game we began to wonder if the Rams hadn't replaced them. The Rams famous "Front Four" (or "Deacon Jones and his Three Musketeers," if you prefer) put the heat on Unitas with their celebrated pass rush. They didn't have much success until after we were ahead 24-14 in the fourth quarter. Bruce Gossett tried a 47-yard field goal. The ball hit the crossbar and flipped over. Had it flipped under or around, we would have won the game. A few minutes later, the Deacon and his buddies hit Unitas just as he was preparing to throw and the ball fell short — right into Mr. Maxie Baughan's (Brother Baughan at FCA meetings) greedy mits. Roman Gabriel found Bernie Casey in the end zone and before you could say "wham the Rams," the score stood 24-24.

Just before the game's end, Unitas threw to Willie Richardson. Clancy Williams grabbed it right out of Willie's hands — the officials called it a "steal," but it looked like an interception. The terminology doesn't matter since we never gained possession again.

We retreated to the dressing room and counted our casualties. From this and past games, we had lost Orr, Alvin Haymond, Mike Curtis, and Jim Parker. Fortunately, Unitas and I were still healthy. However, I didn't read or hear any remarks that the Colts' future depended upon my staying healthy.

Trouble sometimes comes double, as we found the next week when the year in — year out troublesome Vikings tied us 20-20. We lost Raymond Berry for the season when his shoulder was injured late in the game. When Unitas was told he had set an NFL record by completing his 2,119th career pass to Berry in the first half, he said, "But we didn't win. That's what counts."

We won our next two. Then the Packers came to Baltimore.

Because of the new divisional alignment, they were appearing only once on our schedule instead of twice as in past years. I thought they got out of our division just in the nick of time.

Coach Lombardi attended eight a.m. Mass at St. Ignatius Church in downtown Baltimore and learned how far the Colt spirit had infected Baltimore. The priest said from the pulpit, "Even though Coach Lombardi of the Packers is with us here this morning, we ought to remember the Colts in our prayers."

But for three quarters and most of the fourth heaven seemed to smile on Lombardi who wanted to increase his win streak to eight out of ten over Don Shula. The Colts under Shula held a winning record over every other NFL club except the Packers.

With 2:22 remaining the Pack led 10-0, with three points from a 50-yard field goal by Don Chandler.

Then Unitas picked up six points on a pass to Alex Hawkins. Because Bobby Boyd had been put out with a separated shoulder, the Colts had to use a substitute holder for the point-after kick. First-year man Rich Volk put the ball off the spot and Lou Michaels' kick went wide. Behind 10-6, a field goal woudn't tie.

Michaels kicked "onside," and Volk redeemed himself by re-covering the ball. Unitas moved the offense to a first down, then threw to Willie Richardson on the two. Willie shook off the claws of Herb Adderly and went in for the winning points.

Baltimore smiled that night; the Colts had broken the Packer jinx — and the fans kept on smiling as we won our next four games.

Now only the Rams were left. They had beaten Green Bay in a heart-stopper the week before. A win or tie would send us into the play-offs by virtue of scoring more points in the two games.

The big question was: Could we win with the second and third-stringers who had replaced injured starters Jim Parker, Raymond Berry, Jimmy Orr, Mike Curtis, Bobby Boyd and Lenny Lyles? Parker had announced his retirement after the last game so a healthy player could take his place on the roster. Don Shula hit the nail on the head when he said, "We don't really have spectacular players, but our team works toegther."

The Rams came into the game feeling high, after having beaten Green Bay the week before.

For a few marvelous minutes we led 7-3, then Gabriel blew his horn and turned our title dreams into nightmares. He shot us down with three touchdown passes and the Rams' "Fearsome Foursome," led by Deacon Jones, pummelled Unitas for seven losses. When the Deacon spilled John on the four-yard line near the end of the game, he was so pleased with himself that he held both arms over his head and shook his fists. The Rams won 34-10.

Raymond Berry saw limited action with a knee injury that kept him out most of the season.

I have no excuses. I played as hard as I had ever played, and I'm sure my teammates did also. I made 7 tackles by my lonesome and was in on 12 more.

However, the defeat didn't sting as much as the knowledge that because of the new divisional arrangement, teams like Dallas, Green Bay and Cleveland could lose four or five games and still be in the play-off. We had lost only this one game to the Rams.

Don Shula and Ram Coach George Allen tied for "Coach of the Year" honors in the voting of an Associated Press panel. I'm sure Coach Shula would have traded his title for a one-point victory over the Rams.

We flew back to Baltimore to watch the play-off games on television. Green Bay beat the Rams for the Western Conference title. Dallas won over Cleveland for the Eastern Conference title. The Cowboys and Packers played at Green Bay in the "Eskimo Bowl" with the temperature 14 below zero for the NFL title. The Packers won in the closing minutes and earned the honor to represent the NFL in the Super Bowl where they beat the AFL champion Oakland Raiders. As I watched these games, I kept thinking of what might have been for the Colts if we had only beaten the Rams in our last game of the season.

However, in reflecting on the past year I found much to be thankful about. Spiritually, 1967 had been a big year for the Colts. Pre-game chapel attendance had risen to above thirty. Ten to twelve couples had attended the weekly Friday night Bible studies. Seven Colts had given time to speak for Christ:

Raymond Berry, Bob Vogel, Dale Memmelaar, Fred Miller, Bill Curry, Willie Richardson, and I.

I thought of the poem,

> "Only one life, will soon be past;
> Only what's done for Christ will last."

Many Baltimore fans remember me most for this fumble recovery in the play-off with Green Bay for the 1965 conference title. With only one good arm, I ran it back for the first touchdown of my pro career.

17

"Oops!"

I'm not superstitious, but for awhile it looked as if '68 wasn't going to be my year. Our middle son, Josh, was hit by a car in North Carolina while our family was attending the FCA camp there. Marsha had taken the boys shopping and Josh was running across the parking lot when a lady hit him.

I was playing with some high school and college guys when someone rushed up with the news. I went immediately to the hospital where Josh had been taken. Whew! I was really relieved to find he wasn't critically injured. The main injury was a gash three inches in diameter just above his kneecap. No ligaments, cartilage, or tendons were torn. Later we took him to the Colts' team doctor who told us, "He can still play football or any other sport." Josh now has a cross-like scar which we hope to have covered by plastic surgery.

Then my old sidekick and on-the-road roommate, Raymond Berry, retired. He said, "It may be that your body reaches a point all at once where you are more prone to injury, and it seems to me that I have probably reached that point."

Raymond's NFL pro football record stood at 631 pass receptions for 9,275 yards. He scored 68 touchdowns.

Raymond went to work for Tom Landry and the Cowboys as an assistant coach for the offense. The *Tribune's* Cooper Rollow wrote that Raymond's tutelage of Cowboy pass receiver Bob Hayes "marks the greatest blend of talents since a fellow crossed a rooster with a racing form and got a hen that laid odds."

We miss "the man with a million moves" as a player, a morale booster, and as a Christian leader on the team.

Finally, I broke a cheekbone (not from talking too much,

thank you) the first week in training camp and missed two pre-season games.

For the twelfth straight year I made the defensive starting lineup. When there was speculation about my future, Don Shula told a Baltimore writer, "We kid him about his speed, but Don is actually very quick for a few steps at a time. When he first makes his move he's quick, and he has tremendous instincts. That's why he's always around the ball. He's one of the best of the veterans at reading the quarterback's eyes. And he has great hands. When he gets a shot at an interception, he usually makes it. He makes the big play."

Thanks, Coach! Now I'll be waiting for you to say that again for '69.

Someone's computer figured out at the start of the season that the composite NFL player is 6'2", weighs 223.3 pounds, is 26.6 years of age, and has 4.11 years of pro experience. The closest I came to that was in the weight division where I hovered between 215-18, about 15 pounds below my old bulkage.

Two weeks before the first league game, I looked around for familiar faces. Only Ordell Braase in the defensive line, John Unitas, Lenny Lyles, Dick Szymanski, and myself were still around from the '58 squad. Two newly acquired Colt players were familiar from opponent squads. Tim Brown (a ten-year veteran) had come from the Philadelphia Eagles where he had piled up 12,049 yards rushing and Earl Morrall from the Giants, his fourth club since joining the pro game in 1956, the same year Unitas came to the Colts. I knew Earl since the time he had quarterbacked Michigan State in the Rose Bowl against UCLA. The Giants had Tarkenton, a scrambler, and presumably had traded Morrall, a classic pocket passer, because he was not in their mold. None of us expected Earl to be a starter on the Colts so long as Unitas stayed healthy. He was on the squad as fire insurance. Also, Jim Ward, our second string quarterback was out with an injury.

The veteran Baltimore sportswriter Cameron Snyder looked us over and said that with Unitas we had the best balanced team since 1958, the last year we had won the NFL title. Without Unitas, he said, we could play at least .500 ball.

Pro Football Weekly picked us to finish behind the Rams again with the Cowboys playing the Oakland Raiders in the Super Bowl. *Look* also put us behind the Rams in the Coastal Division, and predicted the Rams and Raiders would meet for the world championship.

We planned on proving these and other prognosticators wrong. We were particularly determined to finish ahead of the Rams, who had bumped us in '67.

The exhibition season ended with a discouraging 16-10 win over the Cowboys. I say discouraging because Unitas' "tennis elbow" and pulled muscle forced him out after one series of downs in the fourth quarter. He had completed 12 of 22 passes, but some of his throws had been way off their mark.

The next week when the Colts opened against the 49'ers at home, Unitas did not start — the first time since 1957 when the Colts opened a season without him at quarterback. Earl Morrall stepped in to pilot the Colts against the first of four teams for which he had played before coming to the Colts.

Earl's second pass was batted into the arms of the 49'ers defensive end Stan Hindman who ran it back 25 yards for a touchdown. Earl said later, "I felt miserable." But Earl had been around long enough to know that one play doesn't make a football game. Playing conservatively, because he hadn't yet learned everything about our system, he threw two touchdown passes. This plus two Lou Michaels' field goals and a one-yard run by Tom Matte gave us a 27-10 win and proved that we could win at least one without our No. 1 player.

The next week Jimmy Orr caught his first professional pass in his hometown of Atlanta as Morrall directed the Colts to a 28-20 win. John Unitas stood on the sidelines with his sore elbow and fed Earl tips whenever the ball changed over to Atlanta. It was a touching sight to see John giving his substitute advice. Unitas never stood greater in the eyes of the Colts.

I pulled a muscle in the third quarter, but played with it until almost the end of the game. I have a saying: *If you can walk, you can play.*

However, the muscle pull kept me out of the next four games, of which we won three, lost one. I began to understand how

Unitas felt while watching the play from the sidelines.

For the record, here are the scores of those four games:

Colts 41 — Steelers 7. (Another of Morrall's old teams.) Get this — the defense scored three touchdowns on interceptions. Bubba Smith, Baltimore's tiny 295-lb. defensive end, deflected two of the passes into his teammates' hands. Over in Minneapolis the Bears lost two quarterbacks, Bukich and Concannon, to injuries the same day.

Colts 28 — Bears 7. The Bears' rookie quarterback Virgil Carter couldn't handle the Colt defense. For the fourth straight game, the Colt offense gained over 100 yards on the ground. Gale Sayers accounted for the Bears only touchdown. I watched him streaking down the field and wondered what would happen to the Bears if they lost him.

The Rams also won their fourth straight and kept the pressure on us.

Colts 42 — 49'ers 14. Preston Pearson, a second-year Colt who had played nothing but basketball in college, ran the opening kickoff back 96 yards. Rich Volk ran an interception back for 90 yards. But the big news was John Unitas. Coach Shula sent him in for "experience" and he looked good.

I'd just as soon forget the next game: Colts 20 — Browns 30. Don Shula started Unitas in the second half, and poor John completed only one of 11 passes and had three interceptions, two of which the Browns ran back to set up scores. However, we couldn't blame the loss entirely on John's sore arm. Some of his interceptions were due more to bad breaks than to bad throwing. Leroy Kelly, who had played for Morgan State College in Baltimore, ripped off 130 yards in running and scored twice. Man, did we itch to get at that guy again.

The Rams kept right on winning and moved a game ahead of us. They were our next opponents when I returned to the 40 man squad.

We had to win it and did — 27-10. The Rams' highly publicized front four got to Earl Morrall only once while our defensive line kept Roman Gabriel moving in reverse. Tom Matte and Jerry Hill rushed for 159 yards. Earl passed for two touchdowns and ran for a third. The Rams defensive leader Maxie

Baughan was quoted as saying afterward, "They came to play and we didn't. It's as simple as that." Coach Shula chose not to start me in the next two games. I did not start in the Ram game either.

Hey! Hey! Earl led us to a 26-0 victory over his old buddies in New York. Not since 1953 had the Giants been shut out. Fancy Fran the Scrambling Man couldn't get his eggs out of the pan. He got a first down only once out of six third down tries.

A writer saw John Unitas helping Don Shula coach Earl Morrall and called Earl "pro football's first successful heart transplant."

Naturally people wanted to know when John would be back at his old position. Our trainer, Ed Block, said he thought John was over the hump and would be available for limited duty in the next couple of games. Ed, who has helped train the astronauts and has a bundle of degrees, described John's *tendonitis* as "an inflamation on the inside part of the elbow caused by too much strain." The strain, Ed said, was due to repeated snap of the elbow on the follow through of pass deliveries.

Ed noted that John's second trouble spot was *tenosynovitis* involving the sheaths that surround the tendon at its juncture with the bone. The sheaths had become inflamed and caused more swelling. Also John had a growth on one of his bones.

Added to these problems, Ed said, were strained triceps, the three muscles used in the back of the upper arm when John threw straight ahead, and strained muscles in John's throwing forearm.

Ed admitted that all he could do was increase circulation to the affected areas by using heat and cold and massages to stimulate the flow of blood.

But John Unitas stayed on the bench and Earl Morrall, who had become known as "super-sub," continued calling signals.

November 10, we beat the Lions 27-10. Preston Pearson ran a kickoff back 102 yards for our first score. Earl passed for 249 yards but didn't throw for a single touchdown. Still the victory gave him a 4-0 sweep over the four clubs that had traded him off. This was the Sunday when the Bears lost Gale Sayers for the season with a knee injury. It's tough when a team loses half its offense. We in Baltimore were very thankful for the depth and quality of our back-up men.

The next Sunday we beat St. Louis 27-0. Morrall threw three touchdown passes, the last a one-foot lob to Tom Matte. The Cardinals Coach Charlie Winner, once a Colt assistant coach, said, "I helped teach all those defensive backs, except Rich Volk. They were just too good for us." Charlie's quarterback Jim Ray Hart noted that we had shut them out and said, "No other defense has done that this year."

While we were winning, the Rams dropped a half game back by virtue of a 20-20 tie with the 49'ers. The Bears lost their third quarterback, young Virgil Carter, and maybe set a record in misfortunes. The Oakland Raiders beat the New York Jets with two touchdowns in a nine-second span during the final minute and, after NBC switched to the children's program *Heidi*. An avalanche of telephone protests blew out the switchboard at NBC headquarters. A letter writer asked *Pro Football Weekly*: "Who drafted Heidi?" The answer: "NBC picked Heidi first in 1968. She plays left out."

The Vikings fell to us 20-9. Earl was sensational, completing 13 of 16 passes. Over in the AFL the Jets looked like Super Bowl prospects as Namath carved up the San Diego Chargers' defense.

We blanked Atlanta 44-0. John Unitas came in near the end of the third quarter and completed five of ten passes, two for touchdowns. Afterward, Don Shula said he was "encouraged" by John's performance. But John said, "My elbow didn't hurt anymore than it has, but I was like a first grader. Timing is the big thing. You can only get that by playing."

Up in New York, the Jets clinched the AFL Eastern Conference championship. Don Maynard surpassed Raymond Berry's pro record for pass reception yardage. The Cowboys and the Browns had already sewed up the titles in their respective Capital and Century Divisions.

This left the AFL Western Conference (Oakland and Kansas City each had 10-2 records) to be decided plus the Central and the Coastal Division winners in the NFL with two weeks to go.

We were anticipating meeting the Rams in a showdown for the Coastal Division title, when the never-quit Bears upset George Allen's team 17-16 in a game that got six officials suspended for forgetting a Los Angeles down. Since we had beaten Green Bay

16-3 the day before, the Bear victory gave us the Coastal Division title. It was like manna from Heaven, but as I told a Baltimore writer, "No team that wins 12 cotton-pickin' games can be called backing into the title."

The amazing Bears stayed in contention for the Central Division title until the last minutes of their last game, but the Vikings took it by beating Philadelphia and finished with an 8-6 record. In contrast we won our Coastal Division with a 13-1 record. Our last win was anticlimactic as we beat the Rams 28-24. We were tied 14-14 at the half when Unitas came in and led us to victory. Ram cornerback Irv Cross said, "Unitas' arm isn't what it should be, but he still has brains. He can read any defense and he always knows what he's doing."

With regular NFL season play ended, the Associated Press poll named Don Shula "NFL Coach of the Year" for the third time in five years. "It's a great honor," Shula said, "but the only way it will be really meaningful, is if we win it all." He knew that we had to win three more big postseason games to go all the way.

Oakland won the AFL Western Conference title in a play-off with Kansas City. This set the Raiders up to meet the New York Jets for the AFL title.

The lineup for the playoffs leading to the Super Bowl then looked like this:

AFL Title
Oakland Raiders vs. New York Jets

NFL Western Conference Title
Baltimore Colts   vs. Minnesota Vikings
(Coastal Division winners)   (Central Division winners)

NFL Eastern Conference Title
Dallas Cowboys   vs. Cleveland Browns
(Capital Division winners)   (Century Division winners)

NFL Title
Eastern Conference winners   vs. Western Conference winners

Super Bowl
AFL winner   vs.   NFL winner

The Cowboys and the Browns played first, with favored Dallas losing 31-20. Cleveland came up with four interceptions that made the difference. Watching the game on television from Baltimore, we received an eyeful of the Browns' offense, powered by Leroy Kelly who gained 133 yards.

The oddsmakers made us a 13 point pick over the Vikings who had won their Central Division with an 8-6 record. Earl Morrall passed for two touchdowns and our left linebacker All-Pro Mike Curtis, ran a fumble back 60 yards for a third score. Lou Michaels' field goal increased our point total to 24. The Vikings got their 14 points late in the game and never gave us a serious worry.

CBS matched with NBC by interrupting their telecast of the game to show the first live television pictures from outer space. About 2,000 football fanatics called to protest. I'd rather be preempted by Apollo 8 than by *Heidi*.

One down and two to go. Now we had to beat Cleveland, the Eastern Conference winner, to stay in contention for the big title and the big money — about $10,500 to each member of the NFL winning team and $7,500 to each of the losers, with $15,000 more going to each Super Bowl winner and $7,500 to each loser. We had also a couple of old scores to settle. Back in 1964 the Browns had whomped us 27-0 to win the NFL title and the past October they had given us our only defeat of the 1968 season.

The game in Cleveland was big for all of us: especially for halfback Tom Matte and offensive tackle Bob Vogel, both Ohio State graduates. Matte rushed 17 times for 88 yards and three touchdowns, tying the NFL record for most touchdowns in a championship game. Tom came out in the fourth quarter and collapsed in the dressing room. He had been kicked in the back and banged in the ribs. The Colt doctors said he had a slight concussion and contusion of the lower back but would play in the Super Bowl. Bob Vogel played the whole game with a wrist in a cast. As we say in Baltimore, *If you can walk, you can play*.

The Browns became desperate in the third quarter and threw in old pro Frank Ryan for Bill Nelsen at quarterback. Frankie boy pulled away too fast from under center on the first play, leaving the snapped ball fluttering around like a wounded bird.

I said, "Come to papa, Sweetie," and grabbed it on the 20-yard line. This led to Lou Michaels' second field goal, which added to Cleveland's humiliation. Final score: 34-0. I think Leroy Kelly made 28 yards in 13 carries.

Joe Namath and the Jets trimmed the Oakland Raiders 27-23 and won the AFL title. They say it was like Kennedy Airport at five o'clock on Friday afternoon. Namath threw 49 times and Daryle Lamonica, the Oakland quarterback, passed 47 times — a total of 96 passing plays. Don Maynard was the key Jet receiver with 118 yards and two touchdowns. He made a sensational 52-yard catch which set up the Jets final go-ahead score.

The Jets gave the game ball to Coach Weeb Ewbank, the ex-Baltimore coach who had directed the Colts to NFL titles in 1958 and 1959 against a New York team. Now the tables were turned for an even greater spectacular event with Ewbank pitted against his old pupil Coach Shula and a team of veterans, many of whom he had trained.

We flew home from Cleveland on what else but a jet. The crowd (estimated at 10,000) was so big and boisterous at Friendship Airport that airport police diverted our plane to a safer area. Don Shula gave us three days off to rest.

While taking it easy at home, I noticed that Jimmy "the Greek" Snyder, the sports analyst for bettors, had made us a 17-point favorite with this breakdown: Four-point edge to the Colt defensive front four, four to the linebackers, four to the cornerbacks and safetymen, two to the offensive backs, plus three for the NFL mystique and Don Shula's coaching.

Maybe this and all the articles predicting we would sweep the Jets out to sea helped get them high for this game, I don't know. I heard that Weeb Ewbank gave them a pep talk a few days before the game and reminded them that most of the sports world had tagged them to lose by two or three touchdowns. I imagine he talked as he did to us back in 1958 when we were in somewhat the same position. Weeb is good at getting the pride up in a football team.

The 16-7 Super Bowl upset — and it was definitely that — will be chewed over in sports columns and bull sessions *ad infinitum*. Colt fans will point out that the Jets had the lucky breaks and we didn't. Jet boosters will say that their team could have beaten us without the breaks. For the record, Joe Namath said after the game that two or three plays going the other way could have decided the game in our favor.

On the Jets first touchdown drive, their receiver George Sauer came over my shoulder and knocked an interception out of my hand. John Mackey dropped a couple of passes. Earl Morrall missed an almost certain touchdown when he failed to see Jimmy Orr who was in the clear by 30 yards and was intercepted trying to hit Jerry Hill in heavy traffic. We missed some other opportunities.

Namath put the pressure on my side of the Colt defense. Despite what some writers say, I think I had a perfect game on pass defense. I could have done better on two or three running plays, and I'll admit I didn't have one of my best days in blitzing. To make matters worse, the TV announcer kept calling me "Dan Shinnick"! Where has this guy been during the past 12 years?

After the start of the third quarter, Chuck Noll, our defensive coach, and Don Shula benched four of us on the defense: Bob Boyd, Ordell Braase, Lenny Lyles, and me. Why? — you'll have to ask them. I expect they were trying to get something going. Shula put Unitas in for Morrall — Earl had a bad day, no question about that. John got the touchdown. Maybe if John had gone in earlier, the game might have been different. There are always a lot of maybe's in reflecting on any game. I suppose the best thing to say is that most of us were flat except maybe Tom Matte who turned in some nice runs — and all the Jets were sharp.

We just didn't make the big plays we did during the season. That Namath was the cat's meow. He couldn't seem to do anything wrong. He really made his critics eat crow, especially those who had been calling him "Big Lip." One writer said, "From now on, if Namath says there's a lion behind me, I'm going to jump."

I do want to throw in two bits for our defense. The Jets scored only 16 points on us. Check back and you'll see that the Green Bay defense allowed about the same number of points in their 1966 and '67 Super Bowl games. In our case, the offense didn't score what Green Bay did. Understand, I'm not faulting our offense — the guys did their best. I'm just making a comparison.

Joe Namath was awarded the sports car for being the best player in the game. Personally I think one of his offensive linemen, or Snell or Boozer, or perhaps a defensive back should have gotten it.

I always try to find something good in a loss. While walking off the field in Miami, I caught up with one of the Jets' offensive stars (that was the only time I caught up with him all day), and said, "Good game, but don't leave the Lord out of this." He turned and looked at me and said, "Yeah, you're right." Now if we had won, I probably wouldn't have been able to say that. What's that Bible verse — "witnessing both to small and great"?*

We had silent prayer, then repeated the Lord's prayer together in the locker room. That and the prayer at the end of the last 1967 Ram game were two of the toughest prayers we ever prayed. We also prayed before the Super Bowl this year. Maybe we should have tried praying during the game. I heard after the game that one of the Jets said, "The Lord was really on our side today."

Our team dispersed after the game and we left to lick our wounds. I spoke two nights later in the Lane Adams' Crusade for Christ in Salisbury, Maryland. Then after a few days with the family, I left for some FCA appointments.

I've never liked losing to anyone. But since we did lose in this our first Super Bowl, I'm glad Weeb Ewbank was the winning coach. Sure, everyone seemed to be giving the Jet players, especially Joe Namath, the credit. Joe and his teammates deserve their win. But Weeb deserves a lot of praise also. Just as in 1958 when he coached the Colts, he took a bunch of guys whom many sports experts predicted couldn't win, and they pulled off an upset. Congratulations, Weeb, for this one, but look out next year if you happen to win the AFL.

Naturally, I hope to play my thirteenth season of pro ball this fall. Then I hope to play my fourteenth and my fifteenth and my sixteenth . . . well, I expect I'll have to quit some time.

What then? I am planning on coaching, but I'm not worrying. I'm sure God will have something else for me to do. With Him, I'm always a winner.

*Acts 26:22

Rafer Johnson (seated in center), an old UCLA buddy, was honored on "This Is Your Life." The show closed before they could honor me.

Now if you want a live-wire banquet speaker, call me.

Faces of some important people in the FCA world. Top shows a group at a pro athletes' retreat in Tampa, Florida. Seated from left to right: Perry McGriff, Dave Wickersham, C. S. Motz, Vernon Law, Branch Rickey, Paul Benedum. Second row: Jim Shofner, Mike Brumley, Gerry Craft, Don Shinnick. Standing: Bill Krisher, Bernie Allen, LeRoy King, Tony Romeo, Tom Landry, Maxie Baughan, Prentice Gautt, Dr. Louis Evans, Jim Ray Smith, Carl Erskine, Don Demeter, Jackie Kemp, Hoot Gibson, Clyde King.

I identified the guys in the top pix. See how many of these FCA athletes you can name. To start you off, the guy on Bill Wade's right is Shinnick.

A Christian pro athlete has many opportunities to witness of his faith.

I spoke at the 1969 Winter Banquet for the U.S. Air Force Academy Cadet Fellowship of Christian Athletes. Left to right: Chaplain, Major Alston R. Chace; Cadet Gary D. Combs, FCA president, a Baltimore Colts' linebacker; Lt. General Thomas S. Moorman, Academy Superintendent; Cadet Gary L. Baxter, FCA vice president.

Making the beach scene at Long Island, N.Y.

At FCA conferences, I have the opportunity to counsel younger athletes. This is Jack Waggoner, a high school senior from Lakewood, Ohio.

. . . and FCA guys go to prisons. Here I am walking with Kansas State All-American basketball cager Jack Parr (on my right) and baseball's Norm Siebern (on my left) at Leavenworth Federal Penitentiary. No, they didn't try to lock me up.

"This is a football." At Black Mountain, North Carolina FCA Conference.

I think Rocky Young (lett) was leading a song at this FCA conference. Paul Dietzel (next to Rocky), James Jeffrey, and I must have been checking his technique. The people behind must have been checking on us.

Strong man Paul Anderson is at the mike. I'm at the end wishing I could lift 6,000 pounds.

A volleyball game in the Dogpatch Olympics at an FCA conference.

18

"Press Conference"

For the first time in my life I'm going to hold a press conference. Or, maybe I should call this chapter "Instant Replay" (with apologies to Jerry Kramer who wrote a book under this title,) since I'll be giving answers to questions asked me during the past 15 years. These questions have been asked at such events as high school assemblies, Rotary or Kiwanis groups, churches, college groups, etc.

I'll tackle the football questions first:

Q. What does a linebacker do?

A. I was once asked this question at a ladies' meeting. Before I could get my little mouth open, an old lady said, "He backs up the line." That's true; a linebacker helps stop the runner who might get past the front defensive line. But I'm also thinking pass and how to help the deep defenders. A linebacker's mind must run on two tracks — will the quarterback call a run or pass? — and be ready for either. The three linebackers are in-between the defensive line and the deep backs. They are, strictly speaking, neither linemen nor backs, but a part of both, depending on how the play goes.

Since we're on this business of defining, I'll correct a few erroneous definitions of football positions: Tight end — not a player who has been drinking; split end — not a schizophrenic; tackle eligible — not necessarily a bachelor; ineligible receiver — not necessarily a married man.

Q. How fast can you run a 100 yard dash?

A. Being a linebacker on defense, if I have to run 100 yards after somebody — it's too late!

Q. What has been your biggest thrill in football?

A. When the play goes the other way. Seriously, I can't decide between three big thrills. One, when I ran 73 yards against Kansas, the first time I carried the ball in college. Two, when I stopped Charlie Conerly one foot short of a first down in the 1958 NFL title game's sudden death period. And three, starting as a rookie.

Q. You're number 66, aren't you?

A. No, number 99 — I'm upside down most of the time.

Q. What do you do when there's a fight on the field?

A. Run and get under the bench.

Q. What happens under the pile?

A. Ouch! No, really nothing happens. Only one time did a guy dig at my eyeballs.

Q. Why don't some big-name college players make it in pro football?

A. This could be one reason: Joe College comes in thinking his honors arc a magic carpet to sure success. He's great the first year or two, then he relaxes and stops learning. He finds the third year he can't get along on past knowledge.

Q. What is the greatest asset of a linebacker?

A. Anticipation of the next play.

Q. What do you consider the greatest strength of the Colts?

A. We work well together as a unit. We have a lot of guys who, having played together over long periods of time, have come to know one another's strengths and weaknesses. We do have what the news media call super stars, but some of them are overlooked in pro-bowl selections.

Q. What do you believe is your greatest weakness?

A. I don't have blazing speed.

Q. What excuse can you give for an official giving a bad call?

A. Sometimes he may see the play from a bad angle. That had to be the problem when Green Bay's Chandler was credited with a field goal during our play-off game. The films showed the ball went a yard outside the goal post. Television proves what difference angle can make — a sideline camera will confuse fans at home sometimes.

Q. Who's the best player in pro football?

A. You mean, who's the second best? Seriously, I'd have to answer that by positions, because you can't really compare receivers with quarterbacks, for example. See the next chapter for my All-NFL team during the years I've played.

Q. Who's the toughest offensive player, on a personal basis, you ever played against?

A. Mike Ditka. Mike is as big, as strong, as quick, and faster than I. The only thing I have on him is that I'm better looking.

Q. What do you think about while the offensive team is in their huddle?

A. I try to remember if I made my last insurance payment. No, I think about the team's favorite play from any given position on the field and from any formation, and what I can do to defend against it.

Q. What is your most memorable pass interception?

A. Against Green Bay in 1964 when the interception came in the last minute and saved the game. After that we won 11 straight and the Conference championship.

Q. What color are Joe Namath's eyes?

A. I didn't get close enough to see his number, much less his eyes.

Q. Tell your most embarrassing moment in pro football.

A. Well, it wasn't one of the times I ran from a fight. It was in 1959 just after Unitas threw an interception. I ran into the defensive huddle and Art Donovan asked, "Where's your helmet?" The team had to take a time-out while I ran back to the bench and got my head gear. I guess I was just overanxious. Time-outs are pretty important.

Q. What's the funniest thing you ever saw happen in a pro football game?

A. Believe it or not it wasn't when I called an umpire a quack. It was several years ago when we were playing the Rams who had Billy Wade as their quarterback. We were ahead by three touchdowns very late in the game when suddenly I realized only ten men were in our defensive huddle and Art Donovan was in the Ram huddle. We yelled for him to come back and when he did, we asked him what was he doing in the Ram huddle. He said, "I was telling that stupid Billy Wade not to throw any more long passes because he can't win now anyway, and I'm tired out chasing him."

Q. Do you take a shower after a game?

A. When physically able.

Q. Do you lift weights?

A. No, the good Lord just gave me a 19 inch neck and the body I have.

Q. How long after a game do you think about mistakes?

A. All year. Seriously.

Q. If you hadn't been a pro football player, what would you have liked to be?

A. A mountain climber, although I'm afraid of heights.

Q. What's your formula for making an interception?

A. Be in position where the ball is going to be thrown. Study the habits of the quarterback. Practice catching passes. Study pass patterns.

Q. Why do you talk so much on the football field?

A, I like the sound of my voice. Opponents don't like the sound of my voice.

Q. Was the movie "Paper Lion" really what happens in a pro-football camp?

A. Not in our camp.

Q. What injuries have you had?

A. My only serious injury has been a broken right forearm and four or five real bad pulled muscles. I've also had a few minor difficulties such as a finger dislocation, sprained ankles, sprained left knee ligament, cracked cartilage in the right knee, broken left hand, a slight concussion, and two or three slightly strained muscles. I've had a hyperextension of the left elbow — that's when the elbow goes the other way, and an inner ear infection during a training camp that kept me off-balance for three weeks. Some guys think I'm still off-balance.

Q. Do you do anything unusual to keep from being injured?

A. I'm not superstitious, but I do one thing that so far as I know is unique among players. Just before each game I tape each knee with a figure eight and then add big braces. I can't prove that this has kept me from getting serious knee injuries

— the most frequent crippling injury in football — but the record shows that I haven't missed a pro game in twelve years because of a knee injury.

Q. What is your greatest fear in football?

A. 1. Letting my team mates down. 2. Getting injured.

Q. What's the best fan town in pro football?

A. Naturally, for football, I'll have to say first Baltimore, then Green Bay, then Detroit. But when it comes to sports in general, I'll have to say Detroit. This town supports four major sports: football, baseball, hockey and basketball, and they support them well.

Q. Can a person become too much of a football fan?

A. Yes, if you let pro football or any sport dominate your life. There are some churches that start worship services at 10:30 a.m. in order to get the people out for the football game. There are some fathers who neglect their families and sit mesmerized before the TV set all weekend. Football happens to be the way I earn a living, and I love the game, but I know there are other things in life besides football.

Q. What's your biggest gripe about people's opinion of pro football players?

A. The stereotype that we are all big, strong, and *dumb.* Perhaps some people think mental and physical strength can't be present in the same body. I want to say that almost all pro football guys are college graduates. "Big Daddy" Lipscomb was not, but that doesn't mean he wasn't smart. Anyone who has ever played with or against him can tell you he was. Also, many football players go on to earn graduate degrees. Prentice Gautt, the great halfback for the St. Louis Cardinals, went to the University of Oklahoma on an academic scholarship. He is also working on his Ph.D. Frank Ryan, quarterback for the Browns, has earned his doctorate in math. There are others like these two.

Several pros have done graduate work in theological seminaries. "Deacon" Dan Towler of the Rams, Bill Glass of the Browns, Tony Romeo of the Patriots, Dave Simmons of the Cowboys, and Donn Moomaw who played in Canada are five examples.

I did some seminary study, too. I didn't put myself in the above list — not because I'm dumber than those guys, but because to the best of my knowledge they went to seminary planning to be fulltime ministers. Donn Moomaw and Dan Towler are already in pastorates. I went as a layman to better prepare myself for life. I've found that students respect what I say about Christianity more if they know I have attended seminary.

Ever since I first became active in Christian work, people have been "calling" me into the ministry. I've prayed and thought about becoming a pastor. But my talents seem to lie mainly with football and I think now God wants me to be a Christian coach. I can't see that we'll ever get very far by depending upon just full-time ministers to do Christian work. Not that I don't respect ministers; I do. In 1963 I was an "interim" pastor for four months in a Baltimore church — a George Plimpton in reverse you might say. I did everything regular ministers do except marry people. I learned that the pastorate is no easy job. I'll take pro football any day.

This is a good place to move the press conference to other questions besides football. I do know *something* about other things in life.

Q. What do you think about mini-skirts?

A. They look terrible on some women. It's according to who is wearing them — and how mini! Three inches above the knee-cap is okay. Most pro teams fly United Airlines and this is the standard for their stewardesses.

Q. Why do some players call you "Quack?"

A. Because I call other people quacks, especially officials. The rules allow you to say anything to a referee so long as you don't swear. Swearing can get you kicked out of the game. Once I called a ref a quack and he threatened to kick me out of the game if I said one more word. So I asked him if I could talk to myself. He said, "Oh, all right." So, then I called myself a quack.

Q. Do you always pray to win before a game?

A. Well, I don't pray to lose. I do pray that I will do my best and glorify the Lord.

Q. There are Christians on every team. How is God going to answer prayers from opposite teams?

A. None of us knows if it is God's will for a particular team to win. All of us can pray for God's purposes to be accomplished and for us to accept those purposes. I remember Don Shula saying after the Ram defeat in 1967 which knocked us out of title contention, "The Lord must be testing us for something." As much as I like to win, I have to say that there are more important things in life than winning a football game. Being a good witness for Christ is one and sometimes you get more opportunities to witness for the Lord when you lose. To me, one mark of a Christian is to know how to lose graciously. People who learn good sportsmanship on the playing field are better equipped for Christian living.

Q. Why do you always use Christ's name when you pray?

A. Christ is our way to God. I Timothy 2:5 tells us He is our "one mediator" — our go-between. We know God by first knowing Christ.

Q. In fifteen years of speaking why do you talk about Christ so much and not other things such as war, sex, drinking, drugs, etc.?

A. Because Christ changes people's lives. I could spend hours on these other subjects and still not have the answer — Christ is the answer.

Q. What do you mean by this phrase "knowing Christ?"

A. This is something like marriage. First you become acquainted, perhaps in a casual way. Then you become attracted to this person. Then you make a life commitment. Then you grow in knowledge as you live out this commitment in a personal relationship. As I related earlier, I first knew about Christ as a historical person. Then I became aware that I needed Christ to forgive my sins and bring me into a personal relationship with God. Then I committed my life to Him. Since that time, I've tried to grow in my knowledge of His will for my life.

Q. What is your favorite Bible verse?

A. John 1:12: "But as many as received him, to them gave he power to become the sons of God, even to them that believe on his name." I like this verse because it makes this faith relationship with God so simple.

Q. Are you for young marriages?

A. Yes, but I'm against young divorces.

Q. Are you for racial integration?

A. Absolutely, and right here I want to say that professional, college and high school sports have done more to integrate the races than the churches have.

Q. How can you call yourself a Christian and play football on Sunday?

A. If you're going to ask that type of question, I could ask: How can you call yourself a Christian and do anything that requires physical exertion on Sunday? I call myself a Christian because I prayed to God and received Christ into my life. Today there are thousands of people who must work on Sunday to keep our society functioning. They work because their job requires it. Football is my work. I believe a close study of the Bible will show that we Christians are not under the old law any more, but under His Spirit and grace. And I know that because of "working" on Sunday I have many more opportunities to witness for Christ the rest of the week.

Q. Then, if Christians are under the Spirit, can't we do anything we want to do?

A. The point is that if you are a Christian, Christ has changed your "want to." I could be unfaithful to my wife, Marsha, when I'm out of town, but I don't want to because I love her. The Bible says that a Christian is a "new creation" with new desires. The Christian life is a lot like a wonderful marriage. You're in love so much that you delight in being faithful.

Q. How can you say God is love when catastrophes like earthquakes and tornadoes kill so many people?

A. First, I don't say that God punishes people with catastrophes, even though insurance policies speak of certain events as "acts of God." God allows these things to happen within the natural order of events. Because I'm not a philosopher or a theologian, I won't try to give a detailed explanation. I consider myself a specialist in one field — football. But I do want to say that in God's eternal way of thinking there is no catastrophe in the Christian life. As the Bible says, "All things work together for good to them that love God."* There is catastrophe in our level of thinking, of course.

If you've read the previous chapters, you know that I could easily find some reasons for feeling that God has been angry at me — if I looked at life from purely a this-life viewpoint. We lost several important football games by what seemed to be quirks of fate. In 1967 we had the second best won-loss record in pro football and didn't even get near the title games. This year we had an even better record and lost the Super Bowl. Also, several times I have been benched in my career, without a clear understanding of the reason. Then on a personal level, Marsha and I lost a baby, and as I mentioned in the last chapter, our son Josh was injured by a car. Despite all of these troubles, I believe God is working in our lives for eternal good. Marsha and I have prayed many times to this end.

Q. Do you believe the problems of America can be solved within the present political system?

A. First, I want to say that all of our problems never will be solved so long as the human element is present. To put it another way, there will always be bad calls in football games, so long as human officials are used. Second, I don't say that every part of our political system is perfect, but I believe it is the best system on earth. It allows for dissent, and just as important, it allows for participation. The best political system cannot work well without good people. It's much easier to tear down or sit in the stands and criticize, than it is to get in the game and take a chance on getting hurt.

Q. Do you make a lot of money from speaking?

A. No. The most I was ever paid for a speech was $250 for a sports banquet in Canada. Also, I received $300 for participating on a sports panel a couple of times. My usual honorariums have been $15, $20, $25 and an occasional $50. A few times I haven't received anything — not even travel expenses. Once I traveled over 500 miles and was given $5.00. Another time I drove 120 miles and talked to twelve people. At the end of

*Romans 8:28.

the talk, the guy said, "Thanks a million for coming." He didn't give me anything. I do believe a few church groups and other organizations take advantage of athletes like me who speak. This year, I'm a part-time staff member of the Fellowship of Christian Athletes. For this I receive a small salary, plus travel expenses, much less than I could earn from a secular company.

Q. What type of people have you found hardest to talk to about Christ?

A. This may surprise you, but I've concluded that the hardest are people who think they are Christians but are really not. They'll agree with everything I say. They have sort of adopted Christianity as an extra-curricular interest to be toyed with when there's nothing more interesting on tap. One time I asked a barber what he thought a Christian was. He said, "Someone who isn't Jewish and lives in the United States." I felt like asking, "If I had been born in a garage, would that make me a car?"

Frankly, I'd rather talk to an atheist or some college kid who thinks sex is first and money second in life. At least they half way know what they believe.

Q. How busy is your speaking schedule?

A. Well, when Leighton Ford (one of Billy Graham's top evangelists) called me and I had to turn him down, I knew I was pretty busy.

Q. What's wrong with the church today?

A. Basically, I'd say too many spectators. Also spending too much money on buildings and not enough on involving people in Christian activities.

Q. Do you haggle with the Colts over contracts?

A. No. The Colt management has always been good to me. At last contract signing time, they gave me a two-year contract. I think that's being pretty nice to a player over 30.

Q. Do you like other sports besides football?

A. I like all sports. I like to play golf, handball or paddle ball, baseball, and basketball. I like to watch sports on television. I remember statistics like who led the New York Knicks in scoring last year or what was Mickey Mantle's top batting average. In the American League, I've always been a Yankee fan. In the National, I've liked the St. Louis Cardinals since they won the pennant in 1946. I also like to play chess.

Q. What types of music do you like?

A. Western music is my favorite. I guess I like the whanging sound of the guitar and the violin. But I can appreciate all types of music, although I've been about 90 per cent deaf in my left ear as long as I can remember. Since I'm on the subject of physical handicaps, I'll say that a doctor told me five years ago that my right leg is shorter than my left. He said not to worry since about 40 per cent of the people in America are in that situation. So I guess I really am off-balanced.

Q. What are some more of your likes?

A. I like to paint landscapes. And my favorite kind of food is Mexican. My folks used to take me to a Mexican restaurant in San Pedro every week.

Q. Looking into the future, what would you most like to do when you hang up your player's uniform?

A. I can think of a lot of things I'd like to do. After coaching I think I'd most enjoy living with my family at a year-round-Fellowship of Christian Athletes Camp and being sort of a coach-in-residence.

Q. What does Christianity offer that other religions do not?

A. Four things: One, God as a loving Heavenly Father. Two, Christ as a Personal Saviour who rose from the dead. Three, the Holy Spirit tells you that you are a Christian and is a daily Guide in life. Four, assurance of forgiveness of sins.

Q. What do you think about the Colts going to the A.F.L. in 1970?

A. You still play against eleven bodies. It doesn't bother me.

Q. What's wrong with sex?

A. I've never said anything was wrong with sex. Sometimes sex is entered into at wrong times and for wrong purposes. By wrong times I mean outside of marriage. By wrong purposes I mean for the purpose of exploiting the partner. I don't buy the idea that a woman is just something to get satisfaction from. The Playboy philosophy in particular de-personalizes womanhood.

Q. How can I as a young person keep myself pure in relationships with the opposite sex?

A. Read I Corinthians 10:13. There God promises that He will keep you through every temptation or trial that you would otherwise be unable to bear. The Apostle Paul said he could do all things through the strength of Christ.* This means that you must cooperate with God. Billy Sunday once said: "Temptation is the devil looking through the keyhole. Yielding is opening the door and letting him in." Stay away from the door.

Q. Why are so many young people taking LSD and other drugs?

A. There probably aren't as many as you might think from reading the newspapers. I'd say they're searching for an experience they haven't found elsewhere. Also, today's young people have no real challenges. The tragedy is they may end up hurting themselves and their children. Studies have shown this. The sex and LSD questions remind me that life is very much like a football game. In football you can be penalized for breaking the rules. Likewise, in life there are built-in penalties for violating basic rules.

Q. How much fan mail do you get?

A. Not quite as many letters as Unitas. The most satisfying letter I ever received said, "Mr. Shinnick, I liked the picture and autograph you sent me, but the best part of it was the Bible verse John 3:16. I have been away from God two years, and this brought me back."

Q. Do you eat Wheaties?

A. No, I'm a shredded wheat man myself.

Q. What kind of hair oil do you use?

A. Whatever my wife puts on the shelf.

Q. Are you married? (Usually asked by girls.)

A. Yes, but I have four boys. Our oldest boy might fit you. He's very mature at nine.

Q. Do you want your four boys to be football players?

A. I think I'll train them to become club owners. However,

---

*Philippians 4:13.

whatever the Lord gives them in the way of talent, I'm willing to let them do.

Q. Would you advise a boy to go into football?

A. If he has the talent. If he has the talent to be a violinist, I'd advise that.

Q. What do you think about today's teen-agers?

A. They're great. They get more education these days so they have more to be concerned about. They are skeptical, but inquisitive searchers for truth. They are more aware of what's going on in the world. Ask me again, though, when my kids become teen-agers.

Q. Can't I know God by any other way but faith?

A. Yes, you can look at the stars at night and say there must be a God out there, but that only satisfies the intellect. Putting your faith and trust in Christ satisfies your heart and soul as well as the intellect.

Q. In this book it sounds like you are a pretty good guy. Do you ever sin?

A. Yes.

Q. Where in the Bible is the clearest explanation of how to become a Christian?

A. Acts 11:20-26. Verse 26 says in part, "The disciples were first called Christians in Antioch." The question is, why were they called Christians? Because in verse 21 it says in part, "A great number turned and believed on the Lord." Who is the Lord? In verse 20 it says in part, "The Lord is Jesus Christ."

Q. Is there a difference in becoming a Christian and living the Christian life?

A. Yes, you become a Christian by asking Christ to come into your life by faith. After you have done this then you start living the Christian life. Some ways to live the Christian life are: going to church, studying the Bible, confessing sin, thinking about God, loving people, etc.

Q. How do you know the will of God for your life?

A. First, I think there are two types of "wills" — the long-range will and the every-day will. Second, who wants you to know God's will more than God Himself? If it isn't clearly written in the Bible (which makes clear, for example, that stealing and lying are against God's will and love and kindness are within God's will), you should ask Him. He'll lead you in the right way. If you are in fellowship or in tune with Him, you can distinguish His voice from the devil's.

19

"Shinnick's NFL All-Stars"

There are getting to be more "All-Star" lists in college and pro sports than there are different kinds of cereals. So far as I know all are chosen by committees and groups. My list will be unique because it is selected by a single expert, (Shouldn't twelve years in the NFL qualify a guy to know something?) and because it covers twelve years of pro play.

I'll start with the offense.

My quarterback is *John Unitas*. Who else?

John has been in my thinking the best all-round quarterback in the NFL. He's cool, disciplined, and commands respect and loyalty. When he's in shape, he can slash a defense to ribbons with his passes.

There are about ten types of passes in football — the sideline pass, the hook, the long, the medium, the flare (to the back coming out of the backfield), and so on. Several quarterbacks can throw most of these passes real well. But John can throw them all well.

There may be some guys greater than John with particular passes. Y. A. Tittle is the best sideline passer I've ever seen. Bart Starr is the best spot passer. By that I mean he throws to a spot and the end gets there. Norm Snead and Bill Wade are the best long passers. But John is the best all-around of all the quarterbacks I've seen and played against. I've played against John in inter-squad games and scrimmages and know that he is really hard to stop. (Raymond Berry says John is the only quarterback he's ever known who goes downfield to block after he has thrown a pass.) I feel for the defense that faces him.

John is hard to intercept because he throws the ball just high enough and hard enough to prevent an interception whereas some quarterbacks may loaf the ball a little. At other times he may be intercepted because he has the guts to throw into a crowd.

John goes all-out for everything. This carries over in his personal life as well as in football. Every morning about 6:30 at training camp you can hear him starting his car to go to Mass.

John has often been at his best during the last two or three minutes of a game when the Colts happen to be behind. He goes into the huddle and says, "Well, gang, let's just all work or let's quit right here. All of us are going to work. We are going to score." His confidence rubs off on the other guys and if for example, he calls a quarterback sneak on a third and fifteen, they'll block for him to get the yardage.

If John has a weakness, and notice I said *if*, it is a stubbornness to do things his own way. But then you can't argue with success. Also, some people may think he is too eager to beat a defensive player in a certain pass pattern. Say the defender is an All-Pro and some expert, or John's coach says no one can get deep on him. John will send his receiver deep and try to beat the man. Now that's a competitor!

In 1968 the fans saw another quality of John Unitas that we players knew he had all along — unselfishness. He put his brains and experience to work for Earl Morrall, who quarterbacked the Colts during most of the season. This, to me, is a real mark of greatness. Instead of sulking and feeling sorry for himself, John gave everything he had to the game, even when he wasn't on the field.

For split end, my choice is *Raymond Berry*, five times an All-Pro. No one can compare to this SMU boy as a receiver on passes up to 20 yards and in, although some guys may have the speed to handle the long passes better. As you know, Raymond holds the big records for pass receiving in the NFL. In 13 years he caught 631 passes for 9,275 yards. And he scored 68 touchdowns.

Raymond and I are close friends. We roomed together on the road for almost ten years. He is the most dedicated student of football I've ever known.

Sure, he could fake and pull off moves that looked impossible.

He could dance along the sidelines like a ballet dancer, take a pass, and stay inbounds by inches. But more than any other person I've ever known, he worked hard to develop his talents. He wrote passing drills on his wrist tape and football pants. He did split second time studies. For instance, he knew that for a certain play he had 2.3 seconds to get to a certain place on the field before Unitas released the ball.

If Raymond has a weakness, it's that he doesn't have blazing speed. However, he's faster than some people think and if he was even with a defender on a deep pattern, Raymond came down with it.

I wish him well on Tom Landry's staff as he works with Bob Hayes, Lance Rentzel, and other receivers, except I hope he has to stay home and baby-sit or something when the Cowboys play against me. Just seeing him on the sidelines giving advice to a guy like Hayes, will make me nervous.

For my other offensive end, tight end, I'm having a hard time deciding between Mike Ditka, and the Colts' John Mackey. Ditka and Mackey are real good at blocking and overall pass catching, both on short and deep patterns. Both are great runners after they have caught the ball. Maybe in a year or two, I will put Mackey at the top. Look how he's been doing lately.

For flanker back, my man is *Lenny Moore* who led the NFL in scoring in 1964. Toward the last half of his career he played offensive half-back. He has great speed and is stronger than most people think. He has better than average hands. And he can catch the ball real well. When Lenny was in his prime, I never saw anyone who could catch him after he broke loose.

Lenny is much more than just a halfback flanked wide to catch passes. He can run a stop-and-go gait in heavy traffic that fools tacklers and gives him good gains and he can block. In the '58 and '59 championship games he threw key blocks just before the big touchdowns.

Lenny, whom we call "Sputnik" and "Spats," has attended our player's chapel service many times. He now has a sports show in Baltimore.

For fullback, I have to go with Cleveland's *Jim Brown,* although he has never shown himself to be the greatest blocker.

A defense always had to key on Jim, I mean, be conscious of him. Some seasons he ran 40 per cent of the Browns' offensive plays. You knew he would carry the ball, yet you couldn't stop his strength and speed. Once he broke into the clear, Jim (a former track man) was usually long gone.

Jim has given me plenty of trouble. In the 1964 championship, I missed him on a pitchout and he ran 37 yards. In another game he scored five touchdowns against us. But once we held him to 13 yards on 11 carries. So I think he's done his best and his worst against our defense.

Jim Taylor has also been great at fullback — maybe the greatest in fighting for that extra yard. But overall, Taylor doesn't measure up to Brown in my book. Some of Jim Brown's big records are: Most yards gained rushing; lifetime — 12,312. Most combined yards gained; lifetime — 15,459. Most yards gained, game — 237. Most seasons leading league in rushing — 8. Most touchdowns; lifetime — 126. (Lenny Moore is second with 109.)

My halfback is *Gale Sayers,* who was born near Speed, Kansas. He has springs in his legs and is the quickest man I've ever seen. He gives no quarter and takes no quarter. He's just a tough football player.

I'll never forget a game with the Bears during Gale's rookie year when I was assigned to cover him twelve times out of the backfield. He didn't know it, but each time I had the assignment I was in a cold sweat. Only one of those times did they actually throw a pass to him. He slipped and I slipped and neither one of us got to the ball. Good thing for me that he did lose his footing. He's just the fastest and quickest runner I've ever seen.

Tommy Mason, formerly with the Vikings and now with the Rams, when healthy is my second choice at half back. He could do everything, but is just not a Sayers.

Now let's move to the offensive line.

My two offensive tackles are *Bob Brown* of the Rams and *Jim Parker* who was the Colts' first draft choice the year I was their second choice.

Bob weighs about 300 pounds and has about a 54-inch chest. I've seen him clean out the whole defensive line on one play.

He's the only man I know who can block an end, a tackle, and a linebacker at the same time. At the end of the '66 season, guys who had gained more than 1,000 yards voted him the NFL's best blocker. This guy is something else.

Jim Parker is likewise. While Jim played for the Colts, he was John Unitas' bodyguard. He was never better than in the '58 title game against the Giants where Berry set a record for catching Unitas' balls. Unitas was throwing spot passes right over Parker's head. This meant Parker had to get the Giant defensive end before he got to Unitas. Unitas and Berry received the press raves after the game, but they couldn't have done their work without Jim Parker's blocking.

One of my two offensive guards is Green Bay's *Jerry Kramer* or *Fred Thurston*. It doesn't matter which one. They're both good. They more or less revolutionized pro football by pulling out of the line and getting in front of the ball carrier on end runs. They know when to cut up the hole and when to keep running wide. And they're both very good on pass protection.

Kramer and Thurston were a big plus for Green Bay in the first Super Bowl. They gave Starr time to complete his passes. And they led the play when Jim Taylor ran around end for the first touchdown on the ground.

My other offensive guard is *Gene Hickerson* of the Cleveland Browns. The Browns former first-string quarterback Frank Ryan has completed a lot of passes because of Gene Hickerson who has the ability to help hold the defensive rush back for that extra split second which the passer must have. Gene is also excellent in leading on end sweeps. Gene has led Jim Brown and Leroy Kelly on many a run.

The eleventh man on my all-time all-NFL offense is the great Packer center *Jim Ringo*. Jim isn't the greatest on pass protecting, but on blocking and chopping down the defensive middle guard, he's murder. Ringo is also very durable. I've seen him take a blockbuster blow, lay suffering and turning for a minute, then get back into action. Jim was All-League six of the eleven years he played with the Packers.

Now for my all-time defense:

At defensive end, I put *Gino* "the Giant" *Marchetti*. Without doubt Gino is the greatest pass rusher the game has ever known. I recall one game with the Lions where the offensive tackle hit Gino only once and I think Gino slipped then. I'm sure Charlie Conerly and Frank Gifford remember him from the '58 title game. Again and again, he put the pressure on Conerly. Then when the Giants had to have a first down to run out the clock, Gino led the force that stopped Frank Gifford. After Gino broke two bones in his ankle helping stop Gifford, our offense took possession and went on to "win for Gino." The next year Weeb Ewbank played Gino sparingly during the first few games because of his ankle. Our 4-3 record showed it. Then Ewbank decided to keep Gino in all the time and we began burning up the league again.

At the other end of the defensive line, my man is Jim Parker's old nemesis, *Doug Atkins*. Doug has strength, agility, height (6'8") in rushing the passer, and a never-quit attitude (look what he did in New Orleans last year — and in his fifteenth year!) The Browns drafted Doug No. 1 from Tennessee, but didn't keep him long enough to see what they had. They let the Bears have him and he was one of the biggest reasons for the Bears winning the NFL title in 1963.

One of my defensive tackles is *Gene Lipscomb*. Big Daddy hardly ever missed his man. Maybe his form wasn't the greatest, but he knew how to stack up offensive guards and stop the ball carrier. Big Daddy stood 6'6" without his cleats and played at 288. To give you an idea of how big he was, the late Cecil B. DeMille turned him down for a job as one of four platform bearers to hold the leading lady aloft in *The Ten Commandments* because he couldn't find three other bearers to match him.

Contrary to what some people thought, Big Daddy was not vicious. A vicious man wouldn't help opponents up as he customarily did. I once asked Big Daddy about the Christian life. He said, "I think Christ is the right way, but I have more things to do right now." I felt awful when he died three years later in the prime of life.

At the other tackle spot, I can't decide between *Roger Brown* of the Rams and the unique *Art Donovan* of the Colts, although

Henry Jordan of the Packers did as well as anyone over a span of five years.

Maybe I should say Brown, although I can't fault Art Donovan. Roger weighs about 300. He's hard to fool on rushing plays. He's a great pass rusher, just slightly better than Artie and Henry.

So there you have my defensive line: Marchetti and Atkins for the ends and Brown and Lipscomb at the tackle slots.

Now let's turn to my favorite subject: linebacking. One of my three linebackers is *Joe Schmidt,* who played with the Lions from '53-65 and is now the Detroit head coach. Joe had a knack of getting to the ball. Bobby Layne used to say, "Joe knows what I'm going to do before I do it." Joe made so many tackles from his middle-linebacking position, that a stranger in the Detroit stands might have thought the announcer didn't know any other defensive player's name. Incidentally, the Steelers in Pittsburgh (Joe's home town), passed him up because they thought he had a weak knee that might go bad.

For the two outside linebackers, I'll go with *Bill Forester* who was with the Packers from '53 to '63, and *Dave Robinson* who came to Green Bay the year Forester retired. Forester is one of the strongest LB's that has played the game. He moves as fast as anyone and is very smart.

Dave Robinson came to the Packers from Penn State. He's as fast and as strong as any in the game. He's good at covering a lot of territory and with pass interceptions.

Close behind Robinson and Forester on the outside LB slots I put *Harlan Svare* who played for the Rams and the Giants. Raymond Berry says Harlan gave him as much trouble as anyone. Svare coached the Rams after turning in his player's uniform and is now a coach with the Redskins. For the future I see Mike Curtis of the Colts to be the best of them all; if he is not injured.

For one of my two defensive halfbacks I pick *Dick* "Night Train" *Lane,* who played for the Rams, Cardinals, and Lions. First in NFL interceptions in '52 and '54, "Night Train" was also an excellent tackler.

As "Night Train's" complement on the other side of the field,

I vote for *Milt Davis*. Milt, now an educator in Los Angeles, was in the pros only four years, but two of those years ('57 and '59) he tied for the league lead in interceptions. I feel confident in saying that during Milt's tenure he was the most feared pass interceptor in the game. Bob Boyd of the Colts isn't far behind these two. Boyd was first in NFL interceptions in 1965 and third on the all time interception list.

My all-time safeties are *Emlen Tunnell* and *Jim Patton* who were the Giants deep defenders in the 1958 title game. Old-timer Tunnell played 14 years ('48-'58 — Giants; '59-'61 — Packers) and swiped 79 passes, still an NFL record. This Iowa boy was reckless on end runs and would hit anyone who happened to be in his way.

Jim Patton, a Mississippi product, was No. 1 in interceptions in '58. In both Colt-Giant title games ('58 and '59), Jim kept our receivers from going deep. Without him, I think we might have had another touchdown against them in each of those games. Jim was not the best against the run, but the name of the game is passing.

There you have them, the Shinnick All-Stars. Come around a couple of years from now and I'll probably have two or three changes, although it's hard to visualize anyone replacing Unitas at quarterback, Berry as a receiver, and Marchetti as a pass rushing defensive end just to mention three.

As you see I have not put an AFL player on my team. The reason is that I do not think they have been playing against the best. I do think the following players look like they could have been all stars on my team: George Webster, linebacker, Houston; Lance Alworth, San Diego, flanker; Joe Namath, quarterback, New York Jets.

I hope you were impressed with my humility. I didn't put No. 66 of the Colts on the list! But my wife does, oh, by the way, my all-time coach. I'll tell you after I've coached a while.

20

"How to Be a First-Stringer"

Before I turn the ball over to Marsha, I want to make one more literary tackle and give the summary of some talks I frequently give to youth groups and adults.

This is for people who want the best out of life. If you've already arrived, then skip my little pointers and go on to better things in the last chapter.

1. *Commit your life to Christ.* Our starting center is Bill Curry who once was told by Coach Bobby Dodd at Georgia Tech that he would never advance beyond third-string. Here in Bill's own words is how he became a first-stringer:

"People have worshiped some mighty stupid things — like the sun. Right now I can't imagine anything more stupid than a piece of pigskin, but that's exactly what I did worship. No, I didn't have a little altar with a football sitting there where I'd say my prayers at night. That's about all I did lack in my worship of football. It was the best way I knew to glorify myself.

"I was anxious to play at Georgia Tech where I was planning on impressing people with my athletic ability. Well, it took about ten minutes of the first practice to find out there were other guys a little better than I. I remember telling myself, 'Curry, why are you spending so much time on the ground? These guys must not know who you are. They must not have read your clippings.' I soon discovered that college football is a man's game. I began to see that I was not going to achieve what a man should have in this life just by playing ball."

Bill then attended an FCA camp at Williams Bay, Wisconsin.

"What I saw of myself wasn't pleasant. I realized I had been living a lie. The Christian athletes there confronted me with Christ. I made a personal commitment, but didn't fully under-

206

stand until I got back to the Tech campus. There, Jon Braun, the former national representative of the Campus Crusade for Christ, showed me that to succeed in the Christian life, I must let Christ live through me. That simple truth gave me a new attitude toward football, helped me go from a mediocre to a good player, and more important, opened up the abundant life God has for every Christian. I asked the Lord to help me and He gave me a completely new attitude about the game. I quit playing for myself and started playing for Him. I started getting to practice early and working a lot harder. My feet began to move faster and I became first-string because of what the Lord did for me."*

What happened to Bill? His senior year, he was named to the All-Southeast squad, given All-American honors by the American Football Association, and declared "the best blocking center I've ever coached" by Tech line coach John Bell. Bill's Tech teammates elected him the permanent team captain of the 1964 squad.

2. *Select a career to which you can adapt your God-given abilities.* At one-tenth of a ton in weight, I couldn't be a jockey. I have trouble multiplying 2 x 56, so I doubt if math is my thing. I've felt for many years that I'm best adapted to pro football.

3. *Develop your God-given abilities.* As a pro football player, I must keep in shape both physically and mentally. I can't afford to be lazy, or to goof off. The mental development is extremely important. You look at films, talk to guys about your opponents' strong and weak points, you listen to what coaches and other players say about your strong and weak points, and you study charts about what teams like to do in various situations — like when they take possession on your 40, on the 30, on the left or right hash marks, on third and one when they're three points behind and there's two minutes to play and so on.

Mental development is important in the Christian life, too. You don't have to check your brains when you become a Christian. Know what the Bible says about important questions. Get

---

*Bill Curry's story is told in greater detail in the Zondervan sports anthology, SPORTS ALIVE.

the right answers and as the Apostle Peter said, "Always be prepared to make a defense to anyone who calls you to account for the hope that is in you. . ."*

You don't grow into the Christian life. You are born into it, by a faith in Christ as I mentioned earlier in the book. But after you're born, you need to grow. You grow by studying the Bible, discussing your faith with other Christians, finding your weaknesses and correcting them, witnessing by life and word, and staying close to God through prayer and obedience.

None of us ever reach complete maturity in this life. Like Paul, "We press toward the Mark."** We keep growing in Christ, just as a good football player keeps growing. Frankly, I think the big reason I have stayed in the game for twelve years is that I've always tried to keep a jump ahead on the mental part of the game.

4. *Select your priorities.* Here's a high school fellow who has a car and wants to stay in the social whirl and be a top athlete and a good student. The car may keep him from building up his legs by walking or running. The parties may rob him of sleep and keep him away from books and football. You have to decide what is most and least important, then make your time count. Remember, anyone who succeeds must pay the price somewhere. The scientist spends long hours in his research lab. The successful salesman hits the road while the other guys are thinking of excuses why they can't sell.

Carrying this over into your Christian life, I'd suggest that instead of trying to do many different kinds of Christian work, select and do well that which fits you best. I believe my Christian witness is most effective among athletes. I also believe that the Fellowship of Christian Athletes has the best overall program for winning and developing young athletes in the Christian life. So outside of family and football, I've decided to work with FCA. Other Christian guys feel they can work best through other Christian organizations. More power to them. To each his own for Christ.

---

*I Peter 3:15. RSV
**Philippians 3:14.

5. *Prepare to suffer.* Nothing worthwhile is ever accomplished by doing nothing. You can't build a strong body by slouching before a TV set and eating soft foods night after night. You can't succeed by copping out every time you feel a little pain or get hit by a sharp tongue. The good athletes I know stay in the game when they are hurting. As Coach Paul Dietzel says, "When the going gets tough, the tough get going." Never mind the jibes from sideline sitters. Ignore people who say Christians are sissies. They have never been to an FCA camp and heard some of the greatest athletes in America speak for Christ. Your type of life may be irritating to them. The real sissy is the person who is unwilling to put out for what is worthwhile in life.

You can't afford to quit after losing. When you look at the Colts' record, you can see that we've lost some big ones in recent years, the toughest and most devastating being the 1969 Super Bowl. But I go with John Unitas who said when asked if he was heartbroken over the Super Bowl loss, "I've been playing professional football for 13 years and I can't become heartbroken by one game. We made too many mistakes, but nobody is infallible. There was only one perfect Man and they killed Him at 33."

The bigger the game, the bigger the hurt when you lose. Sure I regret our Super Bowl humiliation, but I'm not going to lie down and die. Nor am I going to hide in a cave to escape the future. My attitude is going to be: I may not know what the future holds, but I know Who holds the future.

6. *Do your best at all times.* That's what impressed me about Bob Davenport when we were roughnecking in the oil fields. He cut all the weeds assigned to him and did a good job while I goofed off when the boss wasn't looking. It's easy to let up. I know. In a game I've said to myself, "Why tackle that ball carrier? Two guys have him already." Then he breaks loose for extra yardage. I remember the '58 Giant-Colts title game and shudder at what might have happened once during the sudden death if I had held back from making a tackle assist. My linebacking partner Bill Pellington had hit Charlie Conerly and slowed him down. I came in from the side and stopped his forward momentum one foot from a first down. If I had stood back

and depended on Pellington, Conerly might have made the first down and the Giants might have won the NFL title.

Maybe you're a boy or girl and thinking, *Sure, I should do my best on big jobs, but I don't have to be a fanatic with everything.* So you sweep dust under the bed in your room. You don't cut the lawn around the edges. You don't throw the paper in front of the door. And so on. I warn you now that unless you make a habit of doing your best in everything while young, you won't do your best later in life.

7. *Be a good sport.* I define sportsmanship as following the rules of the game you are in as they appear in the rule book. If I deliberately hit a guy after the whistle has blown, I shouldn't yell at the official for calling a penalty. If I wreck my car taking a curve at 60 that's posted for 30, I shouldn't yell at the highway engineers, or God's laws of Centrifugal force.

I've said before that I think officials on the whole do as good as they possibly can. They make bad judgments as we all do. But this is no cause for me to bust one in the nose.

I expect a little rough stuff in football, a little piling on, an occasional elbow, things like that. I know that if I hit a guy real hard, his temper may get up and he may throw an elbow at me the next time. I take this in stride.

When I'm rushing a passer and a guy holds me, I may say to him, "Couldn't you use more hands?" or "Hey, buddy, that's a nice block you have there — holding." Of course if a guy comes at me with a machine gun, that's something else.

What I'm trying to say is don't be a sorehead over every little insult or injury. Keep the rules and have a little patience with others. This applies to school, business, marriage, and to every human endeavor and relationship.

In conclusion, the first-stringer that I am talking about is being a first-stringer on the Christian team. If being a third-stringer (and that is your best effort) is what you are okay; but you can always be a first-stringer for God's team. Once again, some ways to be a first-stringer are, study the Bible, pray, go to church, love your neighbor, etc. Why can we be a first-stringer? Because we can ask for God's power — His Holy Spirit to help us.

21

"The Fifth Down"

By Marsha Shinnick

After the reporters have left and the autographs are signed, the typical pro football player comes home to his wife and children just as any other employed husband does. I should say that he comes home *with* his wife if he happens to be Don Shinnick and is playing at home. Usually all of us Colt wives wait for our husbands and then we go out for a light meal.

Really there isn't that much difference between being the wife of a pro football player and the wife of a businessman who's on the road a lot. The Colts play half of their games away, but even for those, Don usually leaves on Saturday and is back home Sunday night. The exception is the West Coast when they play back-to-back games against the Rams and 49'ers and are gone a week.

Football season is actually the one time of the year when the Shinnick household runs on a regular schedule and I can plan family activities. From September to December, I know my husband will be home for dinner every week night, except when he goes to California. As a matter of fact I have never missed a home game, not even for having babies.

Every week is about the same. Monday after a game is Don's relaxing day. He may play golf or we'll do something together as a family.

Tuesday, he begins preparing for the next Sunday's game. He goes to the stadium, works out with the team, and may attend a meeting. Then he'll come home for dinner and look at game films at home for a couple of hours before bedtime.

Don becomes more intense as the week moves on. Although

he doesn't display his feelings, I can tell when he is tense and extremely anxious about the upcoming game. He cracks more jokes and acts silly — sometimes his silliness is not even what I'd call good humor. I accept this as part of football life. Don is by nature a jovial person who likes to kid around. But he's more sober and mellow now than when we were first married.

Saturday is a short family day around our suburban home. Don usually takes the two older boys with him to football practice. While the team is practicing Fred Schubach, the equipment manager, baby-sits and supervises a game of football for several Colts' youngsters on the sidelines. Later in the afternoon Don goes with the team and I don't see him again until after the game, whether the Colts play at home or away.

The toughest time for me is from January to June when Don is out speaking and I stay home with the children. I stay because I don't believe it would be fair to leave them home with a housekeeper and travel around with him. I would feel as though I were missing the greatest challenge of my life — that of sharing their everyday experiences.

There was a time when I resented him being away so much and giving his time to other people. Most of the other players had off-season jobs that kept them close to their families. I had a real battle with the Lord until I yielded to His will. Now — although I don't like to be apart from Don for several days at a time — I have time to read and pray and to work at staying closer to the Lord. I feel as Ruth Graham says about her husband, "I'd rather be with Billy less time than with any other man all the time."

Since I let the Lord take over this matter of Don being away the first months of every year, I've never felt trapped. I've loved being home with my children. And I feel close to Don even when he is away.

Now I'd like to say something about our marriage.

We both come from broken homes. Our parents have remarried and we enjoy good relationships with everyone on all sides. We both grew up near Hollywood where permanent marriages are considered a bit unusual. I think it's significant that we had our first little date after seeing a film titled, *Time and Eternity*. Both of us then wanted a marriage that would last.

Yet Don and I are quite different in our personalities. He is outgoing, extroverted, and at times can be the life-of-the-party type. He can really turn on with young people. I am more introverted and converse better in small, intimate groups. Yet I was a high school cheerleader, even though I didn't know the mechanics of football until I became interested in Don.

I was in junior college planning to be an elementary school teacher when the police club entered me in the San Fernando Valley Beauty Contest. Much to my surprise, I won. I had more date requests after that, although sometimes I wasn't sure whether the boy was interested in me as a person or in me as the beauty contest winner.

Because Don was a well-known athlete, I had heard about him before I enrolled at UCLA. At the time I entered college Don was chairman of a group called Campus Crusade for Christ. I was unaware of this when a girl friend of mine invited me to attend one of their meetings. I really went out of curiosity. I was then an Episcopalian, but had also attended the Catholic church quite a bit. I sang in the Episcopal choir and went faithfully to communion, but still felt something was lacking in my life. Perhaps I went to the Crusade meeting hoping to find a greater religious reality. As I look back now I can see how God was leading me to a spiritual awakening that was to answer many questions about life, God and myself that I had pondered since childhood. I am completely convinced that God answers those who truly seek Him.

My first impression of Don was that he was a big, rather sloppy football player. He was clean, but dressed as though clothes were just something you covered up with. He was completely unconscious of men's fashions. At this time, I was impressed with material things and status in the boys I dated — how they dressed, the kind of car they drove, their campus prestige, things like that.

What attracted me to Don was that he was a big name football player. The girls who dated athletes at UCLA were talked about and had prestige.

Then as I came to know him better, I was attracted to his individuality. He was different from anyone I had ever known. His eyes — they're light brown — sparkled when he talked about Christ in a personal way. I could tell that his faith was real and that he knew God in a way I didn't. At the time I wanted to believe. I wanted something real. Don became the person the Lord used to show me that reality could come only through a personal faith-commitment to Christ.

The way I came to really believe wasn't very dramatic. Don and I drove up to the Forest Hills retreat home and heard Dr. Robert Smith, a Christian college professor. After his talk, I slipped into a chapel to pray by myself. I don't remember what I said. I didn't know the Christian lingo. I just wanted to be close to God. Then as we were driving home, I said to Don, "Why can't more people be like this?" The Christian life was all so new to me at the time. Now I realize it was the beginning of spiritual reality.

A little after we became engaged, Don gave me a mink stole instead of an engagement ring. I think he was reacting to so many broken engagements on campus where rings had been given. He said, "Most girls get a mink stole after they're married. I want to give you one now." He did become a little more sentimental before we were married and bought me a ring. Some people think he's big and tough, and completely care-free and relaxed about life, but I know that he's really very emotional and sentimental about personal relationships. He just doesn't show his emotions when among people.

Truthfully, I never realized how beautiful and wonderful and challenging marriage could be until Don and I became man and wife. I still feel that way and I'm sure he does too.

Now after twelve years and four children, I feel more strongly than ever that our relationship with the Lord has been the most significant factor in building our own relationship. I have seen how God through Christ can take two people who share a love for Him and desire to have a Christ-centered home and work through them to accomplish this. I have seen God take two individuals, each with a great deal of immaturity, selfishness and stubbornness and create a beautiful marriage relationship filled with a love that is from God. We prayed together before marriage. We still do — Don and I and also with the children. We can't always pray and read the Bible together daily because of his schedule. But we can have our individual quiet times with the Lord even when we're apart. We both feel that a close relationship with God precedes closeness between ourselves.

Yes, there have been times when we were too busy to pray and read the Bible together as a family. In looking back I can see where problems have piled up simply because we haven't committed them to the Lord.

And, as Don has already written, we have had times of crisis. The biggest crisis was when one of our twins, our first Peter, died from the staph infection. I believe the Lord prepared me for this shock while I was in the hospital. I didn't cry at all when Don told me. I had never felt sure that little Peter would be coming home.

The next biggest crisis came last June when Josh, next to Joel our oldest, was hit by a car in a shopping center parking lot. Don has written about that also. I felt terrified when it happened, but after the initial shock the Lord gave me strength to be calm. Both Don and I are thankful that the injury was not worse.

We're proud of each of our four boys, Joel, Josh, little Peter and Adam. They're each quite different from one another, created with God-given abilities and talents. Joel is a deep thinker, sensitive, loves music and has a tremendous talent for mechanical construction. Josh is eager to learn, loves books and is extremely well-coordinated. Peter seems to be a combination of his brothers and tends to favor his father in stature. He has been an extremely happy child. Each of them seems to be interested in most sports. On Adam we will have to wait and see.

Both Joel and Josh are old enough to be aware that their father is something of a hero figure to other boys. I have tried to stress that playing football is what God wants their father to do and that they too have a special ability for a job in life.

I want them to be like him in their Christian character and emphasize this above all. They are as much aware of their daddy telling people about Jesus as they are of him playing football.

I take the older boys to the games in Baltimore. We have the same seats every year, high up in the upper level next to Dorothy Unitas and Mary Sandusky. The three of us have been sitting together for the last six years.

I socialize with the wives of other players much as the wife of a young businessman would mix with the wives of her husband's associates. We have baby showers and parties. Although neither Don nor I drink, we see nothing wrong with attending parties where alcohol is served. We don't want to become known for what we are against, but for what we are for.

I'm closer to some Colt wives than others, which I believe is natural. Some have husbands active in the Fellowship of Christian Athletes. Some do not. Some are Protestants. Some are Catholics. I've never sought to choose friends just on the basis of like beliefs.

However, I enjoy a special spiritual affinity with the wives who meet on Wednesdays for home Bible study and who meet with husbands for Friday night couples Bible study. These "small group" sessions have been a big help to my spiritual growth. Also, Don and I attend at least one Fellowship of Christian Athletes conference together each year where I enjoy fellowship with the wives of other Christian athletes. No, I haven't gone with him to Daytona Beach yet!

Now after twelve years I believe I'm fairly well adjusted to being the wife of a celebrity. I don't mean that Don is as big a name as John Unitas, but he's pretty well known around Baltimore and a few other places. I don't blush or show surprise when people shove papers in front of him to sign when we're eating in a restaurant. But I will admit that I was up in the stars during the first year or two of our marriage. I still see him as a great individualist — a non-conformist, something which I admire greatly about him, although I don't always agree with him.

I know that Don's celebrity days as a member of the Colts are numbered. He can't go on playing forever. When he does hang up his No. 66 jersey, and assume another role in life, our marriage will still be exciting, romantic, and challenging. I'm sure it will because we have Christ and one another.

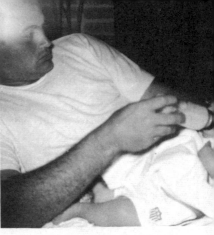

Happiness is marriage to a
beautiful Christian girl;
holding the football—I mean
the bottle—for a young rookie,
and ten years later at a
banquet in Baltimore.

It's a picnic in the backyard with a group of teenagers from church, and five people who love each other in one household. In the family group picture, Peter, our youngest before Adam was born, is between my knees, Josh sits on the floor, and Joel, our oldest, leans over my shoulder. It's our baby Adam with his brothers.

"POSTSCRIPT"

Marsha was right. I have hung up my playing jersey and now wear a coach's uniform for the Chicago Bears.

My lifetime goal has come to reality. Ever since my first year of playing pro ball, I have studied to be a coach. This is one reason why I never took a regular job during the off season, as many ball players do.

I bowed out as a Colt the same year this book was published. I ripped a muscle and had to sit out four games during the 1969 season. After the muscle healed, they kept me on the bench. I felt I had been put out rather than beat out. So with four games left, I resigned.

Naturally people speculated about hard feelings. There wasn't a fight. I didn't go sulking off to hide. I just felt it was time I stepped out as a player. Every player knows his career has to end sometime. I'm just thankful the Lord allowed me to play thirteen years.

The Colts and I parted amicably. Their only regret was that they couldn't win the championship without me.

Besides the city falling apart, there were a lot of other changes in Baltimore after I left. Don Shula went to Miami as coach and general manager of the Dolphins. He got quite a deal there. Naturally this stirred up a whirlwind of wonder over who would get the Colts' head coaching job. I had the privilege of being interviewed for that job. Then a call came from the Bears.

I asked the Bears for a little time. I called Mr. Rosenbloom at Baltimore to see where I was on his list. He said I wasn't number one or two. So I accepted the Bears' offer.

Chicago has always been my kind of town. My dad used to like it here. The Bears always sell out every year, even after they've had a losing season. Papa Bear Halas, the owner and former head coach, is to pro football what George Washington is to America. The Bears is a good organization to work for. They don't have a reputation for firing coaches every year.

From Head Coach Jim Dooley on down, the coaching staff is a swell bunch of guys. Each man on the staff has a specific responsibility. As the defensive backfield coach I'm responsible for the linebackers and deep backs on passing and running plays. Abe Gibron, the defensive line coach, handles the linemen. Most pro clubs have three defensive coaches; one for the linemen, one for the linebackers, and one for the backfield. With the Bears, I coach two positions: the linebackers and the backfield. Some people wonder why there are four offensive coaches and only two defensive coaches. My answer is that's because Abe and I are twice as good.

As a coach, I play a different role than I did as a player. There are some things I may not do. But I can still have fun. My players know when I'm serious and when I'm kidding.

As a player, I was only responsible for myself. Here I'm responsible for seven guys on the field, thinking about what they should do in their various positions, whether we should put in a new wrinkle for the next play, if we should try a new alignment, and so on. Pro football is competitive, not only between teams, but also among players on the same team. A coach must be absolutely fair and keep his word.

I've always believed there's more to building a winning team than simply improving mental and physical skills. There must be good relationships between players and their coaches.

So when I moved into the Bears office I asked Mr. Halas and Jim Dooley if I could take each of my players out to dinner. They both thought this was a great idea.

I started with the guys who had already signed contracts. Guys out of town, I called long distance and became acquainted over the phone. Those around town, I took out one by one. Then I came to know something about them, their families, interests in life, and so on.

I don't think one player believed me when I called and invited him for dinner. At least he didn't show up. I called him back and the next time he came.

There are differing coaching philosophies here. Some coaches don't like to get too close to their players. Some business executives feel the same way about people under them. I believe it's possible for nice guys to finish first.

I like to be good friends with my guys. Christ was interested in people as persons, not in just how they could help Him in crowd-feeding logistics, for example. A professional athlete is no different than anyone else. He likes to be appreciated for what he is as a total person, not just as high-priced husk of brain and muscle.

Winning games isn't my primary motive in building friendships. But I think building friendships helps in games won. ˙To win you must have unity. To have unity, you must have mutual respect between coaches and players. Each guy must respect and appreciate the other's job.

I came to the Bears at a good time. The year before the club had won only one game. What happened that year and before is history. I wasn't around, so I have no reason to comment. I do think they had some bad breaks.

We won six games in 1970. Sure, we only came out third in the Central Division, or tied Green Bay for last place if that's how you wish to look at it. But the way I see it, we improved 600%. We'll win 'em all in 1971.

The Colts under Don McCafferty did a little better than the Bears. Too bad they didn't have me playing for them in the Super Bowl. They would have won decisively over the Cowboys, instead of squeaking out a victory.

Marsha and I have bought a house in the northwest suburbs of Chicago, near where some of the other coaches live. Our four boys aren't quite ready for the pro draft, but give them time. Adam, our two-year-old, is going to be something. That boy is strong and big, but not quite up to Paul Anderson, the world's strongest man.

I continue as a national representative of FCA. That means speaking when I can and giving a new chapter a charter. A coach doesn't have the time off a player does. I can't charm so many folks at banquets. Sorry about that.

Chicago has never been a strong FCA city. Several of us in pro athletics are trying to promote it. With guys like Craig Baynham of the Bears; Pat Williams, General Manager of the basketball Bulls; Jim King with the Bulls; Don Kessinger, Randy Hundley and J. C. Martin of the Cubs; and the indomitable Shinnick—how can we miss?

FCA is really moving on for the Lord. Back in 1955 FCA had 256 college and high school athletes in summer camp. In 1970 we had almost 8,000. The budget in 1955 was $25,000. In 1970 it was $1,200,000.

More and more athletes are coming in. We have Tom Landry, head coach of the Dallas Cowboys. Then there's John Wooden from UCLA, who happens to be the best college basketball coach in the country. And Frank Broyles at the University of Arkansas. Raymond Berry, my old buddy from Colt days, is one of Frank's assistants.

Sure, if you look hard enough, you can find some seamy characters in pro sports. There are some bad apples on college campuses too. But there are a lot of guys on the Lord's side. Most pro-football clubs and many baseball teams, too, have chapel services on Sunday. And I've suggested and presented a program to NFL commissioner Pete Rozell that the League have a director of religious affairs. If we get one in football, maybe baseball will follow.

I believe in putting the Lord out front. Let the kids on the sand lots and in Little Leagues see that many top athletes have a purpose in life beyond money and parties. This isn't to glorify any man, or group of men such as athletes, but to honor the Lord who said, "You are the world's light—it is impossible to hide a town built on the top of a hill. Men do not light a lamp and put it under a bucket. They put it on a lampstand, and it gives light for everybody in the house. Let your light shine like that in the sight of men. Let them see the good things you do and praise your Father in Heaven" (Matthew 5:14-16, *Phillips*).